Getting
PAST
What You'll
NEVER
Get Over

Getting
PAST
What You'll
NEVER
Get Over

Help *for* Dealing *with* Life's Hurts

— John F. —
Westfall

Revell
a division of Baker Publishing Group
Grand Rapids, Michigan

Published by Revell
a division of Baker Publishing Group
P.O. Box 6287, Grand Rapids, MI 49516-6287
www.revellbooks.com

Printed in the United States of America

Library of Congress Cataloging-in-Publication Data
Westfall, John.
    Getting past what you'll never get over : help for dealing with life's hurts / John F. Westfall.
        p.   cm.
    Includes bibliographical references.
    ISBN 978-0-8007-2063-6 (pbk.)
    1. Suffering—Religious aspects—Christianity. 2. Christian life. 3. Emotions—Religious aspects—Christianity. I. Title.
BV4909.W47   2012
248.8′6—dc23   2012018538

12   13   14   15   16   17   18   7   6   5   4   3   2   1

This book is lovingly dedicated
to Frank and Laurel Westfall,
who lived the adventure
with faith, courage, and tenacity.
You gave me life and then
encouraged me to live it abundantly.
Mom and Dad, thanks to you
I know who the Shepherd is.

Contents

Acknowledgments

I owe great debts. Not just the usual ones, but the more important relational ones. This book would never have been written without the encouragement and insight of caring friends. Their stories are woven throughout the fabric of this book, and their gifts of vulnerability, accountability, and commitment are priceless. Thanks to Joe Boldan, Jim Eaton, Roger Anderson, Pam Proske, and Darrel Young, who in varying ways came alongside to remind me that God wasn't finished with me yet. I'm grateful for our new family at Harbor Church; together we are healing and challenging one another to go out on the next adventure. You have helped me rediscover life for the adventurous spirit!

Thanks to Lonnie Hull DuPont, who worked on this project with enthusiasm and wisdom, which is a great combination. I appreciate the instincts you showed with every word you crossed out and every idea you clarified. Thanks also to Lindsey Spoolstra and Janelle Mahlmann, and the rest of the Revell team, who helped navigate me through to completion and helped this book become a reality.

Special thanks to Hazel Larson for her amazing editing and relentless encouragement. My debt to you and Bruce may never be adequately paid, but I suspect it won't matter because you both have shown amazing grace to me.

Finally, and most importantly, I love my family. Damian has generously allowed me to share some of his story and has taught me the meaning of courageous love. To my wife Eileen, who has walked this journey with me: there would be no book without you. Thanks for keeping hope alive when we were most broken. God must have known I needed someone who can pray without ceasing.

1

The "Get Over It" Fallacy

It has been said, "Time heals all wounds." I do
not agree. The wounds remain. In time, the mind,
protecting its sanity, covers them with scar tissue,
and the pain lessens. But it is never gone.

Rose Kennedy

W hen are you going to get over it?"
How many times had I heard that question? I
wanted to say, "soon," or "any day now," or "I'm already
over it." I really did. It might make things easier for everyone
else, and maybe it would help me not feel like such a negative whiner.

There were times when I wondered what was wrong with
me. After all, everyone else had bad stuff happen and they
seemed to bounce right back like the inflatable punching
bag I had as a kid, which was shaped like a clown with a
bright red nose. It tipped back when punched, then seemed

to magically right itself. Of course, I also discovered that if I punched too hard it came flying back and hit me in the face with its red nose.

Growing up, I assumed I was supposed to be like that toy: when I was knocked down (figuratively or actually), I'd try to bounce back without letting anyone know how much I hurt. But we are human, not inflatable punching toys. We don't immediately bounce back, and the pain, scars, and bruises in life are real—and they often really hurt.

Perhaps no one wants to hear this, but I'm going to say it anyway: the truth is things happen to all of us that we will never get over.

It took me a long time to finally admit this to myself, and now to you. I've spent a lifetime trying to snap out of it, pick myself up and dust myself off, keep a stiff upper lip, and never let them see me sweat. I believed "things aren't as bad as they seem," and when all else failed I could "whistle a happy tune," so no one would suspect I was afraid.

Popular "Wisdom"

There are plenty of witty and superficial answers and advisers encouraging us to "Get over it." *Good Morning America* even featured a segment about celebrating a national Get Over It Day, based on the assumption that all of us have something to get over.[1] The day chosen was March 9, which happens to be midway between Valentine's Day and April Fool's Day. The originator of the idea, Jeff Goldblatt, explains, "Get Over It Day is the day to finally get over that ex-boyfriend or ex-girlfriend, those stressful school- or work-related issues, any fears, insecurities, embarrassing moments, bad relationships, etc."[2] His website sells wristbands telling us to get over it, and even provides helpful hints like: "If you're not sure what you have to get over, just ask your friends what they're tired of hearing you complain about."

Someone told me about another fool-proof solution. This one pointed out that there are really only two simple steps to follow to get over anything: (1) "Get over it," and (2) "Stay over it." In the music world, even the Eagles command us in song to "Get Over It."

Life is too important and meaningful to be measured and controlled by the pithy clichés of shallow people.

Have you noticed how much of our popular wisdom is really dumb? Life is too important and meaningful to be measured and controlled by the pithy clichés of shallow people. I'm ready for a new perspective that takes seriously the amount of courage needed just to get up and keep living in spite of the wounds, brokenness, and blows the world dishes out.

I'm grateful for the everyday people who have learned to get past the things they'll never get over. Whenever I meet people who are rebuilding broken parts of their lives, it gives me hope and encourages me to find a way to get past the painful experiences I've endured.

Over the years I've met many people who have become my heroes. Their experiences of loss and hurt are all different, yet as they share with me, I find their efforts to get past these things can be an encouragement to all those who are going through difficult times. Their brokenness was often incurred in only a minute, but the shock waves of pain went on and on—and still go on. Yet each one of these people is discovering the power to get past what they will never get over. That gives the rest of us hope to live past the losses we've known.

While we recognize and appreciate fellow strugglers, let's resist the temptation to compare and measure our various levels of hurt, and put away our "pain-o-meters." Say, for example, I suspect my brokenness may not measure up to the degree of hurt you've endured. It doesn't matter what kind of brokenness we've experienced. Is relational brokenness less significant than physical brokenness? Of course not. I've come to realize pain is pain—and it hurts.

In order to get past our brokenness, we must recognize it for what it is and set aside the need for an instant fix. Then by God's grace we can begin the journey toward freedom and joy that can be ours no matter what we've been through.

Not long ago I was talking with a friend in our neighborhood Starbucks, sharing some of the pain and frustration I felt. As my friend patiently listened, I was struck by the emotional intensity I was expressing. In the back of my mind, I probably felt a little skeptical that the future would ever be different. But when I was done unloading, he blurted out, "Aren't you glad you won't always feel the way you do now?"

I thought about that for a long time. When we are in the midst of pain and loss it is natural to assume we'll always feel that way. This may be one reason it is so difficult to have hope. But we aren't doomed to be stuck in our pain. Our lives will change, our feelings will be different, and we'll have opportunities to feel and experience life differently.

Think about it. If a person is doing very poorly, circumstances will eventually change. The flipside is also true: when things are going great for someone and they're on top of the world, that will also change. We don't always have everything going our way. Therefore, when we are down we need folks around us who can encourage us and help us become strong. Then when our change comes, we can be the encouragers for those formerly victorious friends who are now suffering like we once were.

If everything stayed the same, we could justify despair. But in the Bible, God says, "Look I'm doing a new thing, can't you see it?" (see Isa. 43:19). I want to see it, don't you?

When I was a kid, my brother Richard had a few carrier pigeons and I had a pet duck. I named my duck Dudley after the main character in the first book I ever read, *Dudley Duck in the Well*. Sometimes my dad would turn into our driveway really fast, which often made me worry about Dudley's safety and his future health. But I didn't need to worry about the pigeons. At the first sign of our Chrysler station wagon they would fly away, returning a short time later when all was safe and quiet.

Dudley lacked the pigeons' awareness and flying ability. He would often stand in the middle of the driveway, head down, intensely focused on something important like a scrap of soggy bread, and never look up or see the looming threat of the car. Time after time I would run over and shoo Dudley onto the lawn, where he'd waddle around oblivious to the dangerous world around him.

I like to think of myself as being like Richard's pigeons. I feel alert, active, free to fly off on an adventure to deliver messages before carefully finding my way back home to the safe "coop" of my familiar surroundings.

Unfortunately, most of the time I'm probably more like Dudley the duck. My attention gets stuck on some small thing and I keep my head down while I fuss and quack. Soon

I start to become oblivious to my surroundings, my perspective becomes distorted, and I don't pay attention to others in my life nor am I very clear about oncoming threats. It's only by God's grace that some caring person helps me get out of the way.

Are We There Yet?

"Are we there yet?" We drove our parents crazy with that one simple question. The problem is, we're still asking it. Maybe I'm afflicted with "Destinationitis Syndrome." That is the disease of perpetual longing for completeness while experiencing frustration and discomfort along the way. It grips us when we want to get over something, but find the journey too long and difficult.

Michael Yaconelli, in his book *Messy Spirituality*, says it's important for people to admit they are unfinished.

> Unfinished means incomplete, imperfect, in process, in progress, under construction. Spiritual describes someone who is incomplete, imperfectly living their life for God. The construction site of our souls exposes our flaws, the rough-hewn, not-finished faith clearly visible in our hearts. When we seek God, Jesus begins to take shape in our lives. He *begins* a good work in us. He *starts* changing us, but the finishing process is more than a lifetime process. The work of God in our lives *will never be finished* until we meet Jesus face to face. . . . It isn't about being finished and perfect; spirituality is about trusting God in our unfinishedness.[3]

Perhaps it is when we are uncomfortable with our "unfinishedness" that we focus on outward appearance and surface solutions, because they might help us appear more together than we actually are. We can fool some people into thinking we are further along than we actually are. The result of this type of thinking is our culture's obsession with shallow appearances—to the neglect of inner character development.

Shortcuts and Shallowness

We have witnessed the turmoil of businesses and financial corporations that focused on short-term results to give an appearance of success while their true corporate culture was eroding beneath their shiny public relations façade. And in education, the pressure for the appearance of achievement can dominate a school system until the system gets exposed for its fraud and deception. A school district in one of our major cities was recently exposed for widespread cheating on tests. The cheating was done not by students but by teachers, administrators, and superintendents who conspired to falsify scores on standardized tests in order for it to look like their students were improving. Evidently this was done in order to receive millions of dollars in educational aid. From the top down, there was pressure to make things look good. Teachers were encouraged to change students' wrong answers on tests so their scores would improve. Shocking? Not really. Perhaps it's easy to shrug off these incidents because they have become almost normal in today's world.

What about us? Will we overcome the temptation to take shortcuts on the path to wholeness? Several years ago, I led an organization that sponsored a charity 10K run. Each year a few hundred folks would gather on a Saturday afternoon in Seattle, where we would take off on a good run for a good cause. There were people of all sizes and shapes and quite a variance in athletic ability. Each year I was usually the least prepared and most out-of-shape of any of the participants. That didn't stop me. As the race promoter, I was busy talking up a storm, trying to get everyone into a running mindset. I talked trash with the obviously in-shape runners and laughingly challenged them to keep up with me.

One year, as the race approached, I had read in a runner magazine that top runners sometimes indulge in "carbo-loading" before a race in order to keep up their strength. I figured what worked for top athletes might work for me. So on race day I took my son Damian to Philipi's Pizza on the Ave near the University of Washington and ordered not just a large pizza but also a big pasta dinner complete with loads of cheese and extra breadsticks. Stuffed, I dragged myself out into the midday sun, feeling more like lying down and having a nap than running a 10K.

When we arrived at the park where the race was held, I wasn't feeling too good. But if this worked for great athletes it surely would work for me. So I put my discomfort out of my mind and got down to schmoozing people.

I had a race strategy that consisted of running as fast as possible for about 100 yards to get out into the lead, and then finding my comfortable pace and waiting for others to catch up with me. So when the race began I bolted to the front, sprinting ahead of the pack.

They say distance runners sometimes experience "hitting the wall" late in a race, and they have to push themselves forward to finish. I hit the wall at around 85 yards. Not 85 yards from the finish line, but 85 yards from the starting line. The anchovies and pepperoni from the pizza were dancing a tango with the pasta, while the garlic breadsticks were trying to cut in to dance as well. I was a hurting puppy with a long way to run. At around the 1K marker, I had been left in the dust by all the other runners. Even young parents pushing strollers ran by me like I was an old Roman statue. It was embarrassing. I had to get a new plan.

Jogging around a bend, left alone in the proverbial dust, I suddenly became a genius. I took off through the woods, winding my way across the rugged terrain until I emerged on the other side, right in the runners' path. Once I was back on the path, it didn't take long before the lead runners were gaining on me, but I didn't make eye contact as they passed me for what was now the second time. Huffing and puffing, I remained stoic as all the rest of the runners went on by (probably questioning how I could possibly have gotten ahead of them).

It wasn't long before I was all alone again, left to myself and my stomach cramps. I thought if that shortcut worked so well once, it might work well again. So off I went through the woods and back to the front of the pack of runners. When I finally crossed the finish line on this 10K run, I had perhaps traveled a legitimate 3.5 kilometers. I had been passed repeatedly by the true runners who, until they read this account, never knew my secret. I'm not proud of cheating in the race, but I realized how easy and tempting it is to take shortcuts and maintain an image.

Unfortunately the combination of those two things, shortcuts and image, undermines the good possibilities for a life well-lived. Paul writes, "You were running a good race. Who cut in on you to keep you from obeying the truth?" (Gal. 5:7). It is important to realize that our lives matter. Our real lives—not the false images we might project for others to see. I want to be a person of substance, but that will require me to confess my tendency to try to "beat the system," get back to the steps leading to health, and persevere even when I'm tempted to leave the path and go my own way.

My friend Jake is really very thoughtful and caring while cultivating an easygoing, happy way of relating. At first I was amused by his bubbly enthusiasm, but then I started to get irritated, thinking that no one could be that positive all the time. One day we were talking, and he asked if I wanted to know his secret. Of course I did.

He told me that in his business of sports marketing and publishing he had developed a persona that helped him become quite successful. I leaned forward to glean the secret he was about to reveal to me. "I've taught myself how to act like Formica Man," he said. He explained that like the Formica tabletops and counters that were popular when we were kids, he acted as if he were three feet wide and only half an inch deep. "Besides," he said, "I'm shiny, and have a hard shell finish that easily wipes clean."

That got me thinking. At least Jake recognized what he was presenting to the outside world. How many of us are functionally Formica men and women, while at the same time we long to be much more? We are protected from damage by our hard surface and free from care and worry because of our shallowness, but we can't help but wonder if our life could be much more real and significant.

I thought about it, and the next time I was with my friend I asked him if he wanted to know my secret for success. He did, so with hushed tones, as if I were revealing the secret to a lost treasure, I told him that while he might be Formica, I was living my life as a one-of-a-kind, antique piece of distressed, unfinished furniture. At first he looked a little confused, then we talked about how the scars, marks, and blemishes of distressed furniture are actually the very things that give it character and add to its value. Our unfinished condition allows hope that there is more to come, and we realize our value is only going up with every passing day.

Up Until Now

Sitting in the seminar room, I couldn't take my eyes off the artificial hand protruding from the sleeve of the speaker's jacket. He was sharing from his experience of how he approached long-term emotional struggles. As a person who has struggled with depression most of my life, I was open to finding a new approach. What he said made sense to me: "I always say, up until now . . ."

I thought about the implications of those three words. Instead of saying "I'm depressed," I could say, "Up until now, I've been depressed." That leaves the door open for the possibility that in the next hour or day, perhaps I won't be depressed. I realized that I was quick to label my feelings and thoughts in a way that might hinder me from seeing new ways to behave or respond. I started to think of the possibilities:

Up until now, I've been a control freak.
Up until now, I've been angry.
Up until now, I've struggled to trust God.
Up until now, I was a thoughtless friend.
Up until now . . .

Well, you get the idea. Whatever we might have been doesn't need to continue to define us. There is always the possibility we might be different as we go forward in our life. That doesn't mean we will magically or instantly experience change without hard work. But the door is open for healing to begin and new health to emerge.

Healing begins when we recognize our brokenness and see it for what it is.

Healing begins when we recognize our brokenness and see it for what it is. Freedom begins when we understand we can get past the hurts we'll never get over. Life may not be the same, but it will be good and maybe even a whole lot better.

2

Baby Steps to a New Reality

I was feeling pretty good. It was a perfect sunny Seattle day and I was driving my red Miata sports car with the top down. In Seattle we don't get too many chances to do that without being rained on. I was giving my friend Kay a ride to an appointment in Greenlake, just north of the city.

As I drove around the lakeshore, Kay suddenly started looking around with concern on her face. "I think there's a fire—I smell smoke," she said. Dismissively I half-jokingly said that of course there were fires; we were at the lakeshore, and people were probably building fires to cook hot dogs or marshmallows—and I kept driving.

She grew increasingly agitated, insisting that the "fire" was very close. Finally, just to pacify her, I pulled off the road and stopped the car. Sure enough, there was a lot of smoke all around us. I opened the trunk—and a fire was burning in the trunk of my little car.

Kay wanted to call the fire department, but I insisted on putting it out myself. The flames were growing while I pulled out golf clubs, groceries, a tray of frozen foods, my computer bag, and a lot of flaming trash. I finally was able to extinguish the flames with my hands and assorted objects I found in the trunk.

What a mess! I had just bought five pounds of fresh blueberries that had now burned down into a mixture of molten plastic and charred remains of fruit. Grocery bags were burned up, my golf bag was destroyed along with various golf stuff, and even a golf club. My computer was saved, but not the bag it was in. By the time I emptied the trunk and put out the fire I was covered with smoke, ash, and smelled like an old campfire.

Then I thought of my life. So many times I'm cruising along, thinking I'm in control and living large—while I completely miss the trouble festering right behind me. I seem to have a pretty good defense system, so it is easy for me to make a quick response that deflects problems. I am also skilled at finding others to shift blame to. "It's not me—it's them!" I say, or, "If it weren't for them, I wouldn't be in this mess!" Thus I remain in denial about my circumstances, and miss an opportunity to see myself as others see me and work toward healthy solutions.

Seeing Clearly

No matter how I may portray the issues, it is still denial and we all experience its effects from time to time. I'm intrigued to observe how many people are amazingly perceptive—when it comes to other people. They have insight about people's behavior, habits, communication, and foibles. Yet often these same folks are apparently blind to what is happening in their own lives. In order to grow it is important to see what's real in the world around us—and also in the world within.

I believe that the single most important trait of maturity is the ability to recognize reality. This is also the antidote for denial. When we clearly see the realities of our own lives, it is possible to leave behind childish things and thinking.

The Bible says we are like children peering into a looking glass: our perceptions are distorted, but someday we will see clearly, face-to-face. "When I was a child I talked like a child, I thought like a child, I reasoned like a child. But when I became a man, I put childish ways behind me" (1 Cor. 13:11).

Life has a way of breaking into our well-structured frame of mind and forcing reality upon us. When I was suddenly terminated from a job I dearly loved, I felt as if I'd been emotionally and relationally assassinated. I found myself floating in a world of pain, sorrow, anxiety, and shame. Each morning I'd lie in bed telling myself that this didn't really happen, and it was all just a big misunderstanding. Surely the people who betrayed me would realize their error and come quickly to reinstate me. Everything would be fine.

Of course it wasn't fine. They didn't reinstate me, and everything wasn't going to be all right. Life as I knew it had careened off the track and crashed in a fiery pile. We had to relocate across the country, and financially we were ruined. My marriage was tested and stressed and I felt like a hollow shell of the person I had been just a short time before.

Fortunately, we had some people in our lives who loved us and encouraged us as much as they could. But it took a long time for me to look with clarity at the betrayal and destruction in my life.

We all need the perspective of wise people. People who care for us enough to not only listen but also speak clearly into our hearts and minds. The Bible encourages us to speak the truth in love (see Eph. 4:15). I am discovering that to do so helps us to see reality about ourselves, others, God, and life itself. As denial fades away we are free to step out in courageous ways. We can start to take the necessary steps that lead to growth and health.

As denial fades away we are free to step out in courageous ways.

In Exile

Over coffee, a friend was sharing with me about her experience. "Ever since divorce entered our family, I feel like I'm in exile. Even though it was my adult child who divorced, we are all affected—and now I don't know how to act, what to say, how to respond. There are new rules for relating and I feel lost, alone, and powerless to make a difference—I just wish we could all go back to being a family again." Living in exile is not fun.

There are times in our lives when every one of us feels as if we are in exile. Changes in circumstances beyond our control, or even the results of our own dumb choices, leave us in a strange, foreign place.

Exile is that foreign place, the uncomfortable and unfamiliar land where we're no longer certain about what we know and who we are. It's a forced dislocation. We would not consciously choose it, and we hope it will end at any moment.

26

There are literal exiles in our land, people who have come to this country fleeing oppression or persecution in their homeland. Some are political exiles, but there are also economic exiles. Folks who were unable to survive in their homeland seek the opportunity, money, and resources of a new country, hoping to one day return home with the means to provide for their families. Migrant field workers, who harvest our crops for a few dollars a day, can be deported when the harvest is complete.

Even our college students can experience exile. They find themselves in unfamiliar surroundings in order to pursue their education. This fall our nearby University of Washington will be full of students who will struggle with loneliness, confusion, and disorientation. Behind the façade of "Husky Fever," many will drink too much or experiment with drugs and sex as they try to adjust to this new life apart from family and old friends.

Some of us are exiles through unforeseen circumstances: job change, layoffs, unemployment, accidents, or health crises. These events beyond our control occur, and suddenly we find ourselves in a foreign land. We can't seem to change things and we can't stand the way things are.

Then there are relational exiles, people who feel cut off from others, often people they love. They can't seem to find ways to reconnect or to heal the rift. In marriage, the reaction to this exile is often to gaze longingly at the green grass on the other side of the fence, mindful of weeds and dry spots in our own yards. The seeds of envy sprout into resentment and jealousy, giving way to fear and bitterness.

"If only they were different, I'd be better!"

"If only I were over there, then my life would fall into place!"

"If only he weren't so much of this, then I wouldn't have to be so much of that!"

I'm beginning to think that "if only" and "what if" and "I can't" are all the battle cries of a person in exile.

In the Bible we read about the Hebrew people being in exile (see Jer. 29). Defeated, they were taken to a foreign land and surrounded by strangers who spoke a different language, held different values, and ate strange food. They were living in an unfamiliar place, facing the unknown, dealing with the uncontrollable, and thinking it was completely unfair . . . just like us.

In the midst of such seemingly hopeless situations, the prophet Jeremiah brings words of encouragement to help us prosper even in times of exile.

First, remember who has promised to carry you (see Jer. 29:4, 7). Contrary to popular opinion, we are not merely helpless victims being carried by the enemies and forces of life. Even as we go through the loneliest, darkest, and desolate times, the Lord is there carrying us, especially in our times of exile. Psalm 139 asks, "Where can I go from your Spirit? Where can I flee from your presence?" (v. 7). Jesus said, "I am with you always, to the very end of the age" (Matt. 28:20). It is important when we feel abandoned and alone to know that God is right there with us, and in fact has carried us even into exile.

Next we are told to build houses, celebrate marriages, and become a family (see Jer. 29:5). This seems mundane and not very spiritual. What's the point? None of us knows the future, or how much time we have. The bad times will come to an end, and so will the good times. Our tendency is to put our lives on hold and make no plans, because we don't know how long we will be here. Why put down roots if we won't be here for the harvest?

I think I have wasted a lot of time waiting for things to change before I would get started. I sympathize with the Hebrew people. Like me they wondered why they should put down roots, make plans or decisions, or prepare for an uncertain future. This was reinforced by the false prophets whom they sought out to predict a quick end to their time in Babylon; consequently they felt "in-between" and unable to move forward with their lives.

The Lord also says to those in exile, "Plant a garden" (v. 5). This is a very earthy reminder that no matter what our situation, we are not totally powerless. And no person or circumstance has the power to rob us of the opportunity to consider alternatives in life. I talk to many people who feel like they are "in-between." I understand how feeling like that makes it easy to put off living because change *might* be coming—so we sit in exile, waiting.

I often talk to people about plugging in to their church or community, such as a small group or another ministry, to invest time and attention helping others. Too often they tell me they haven't found a place to get involved, pointing out that they don't know how long they will be there, so they are staying on the sidelines. Then one year, three years, five years go by and they are still on the sidelines, watching life go by, missing opportunities to discover roots and growth and family and love right where they are.

We may not have asked for our circumstances, but they do not have the power to keep us from living every single day to the fullest. It is important to start where we are, not where we wish we were. Richard Halverson, when he was chaplain of the United States Senate, was a guest preacher at our church. After he spoke, I overheard a man asking Dr. Halverson if God would be able to use him where he worked. His response was, "Don't worry about whether God can use you where you are. I know he can't use you where you are not."

So plant a garden and put down roots. Make a home; plan a family. Discover the truth that we can be at home anywhere in the world, with any people in the world, because we know the One who carries us and cares for us. I'm sorry to say that I have probably missed out on a lot of good, just because it wasn't what I was expecting or what I had planned for my life.

Baby Steps

Bill Murray played the part of an obsessive-compulsive, anxiety-riddled yet loveable mental patient named Bob in the movie *What About Bob?* His psychiatrist (played by Richard Dreyfus) told him all that was needed for recovery was a grasp of the "Baby Steps" theory of psychology. We all laughed knowingly as Bob shuffled through the movie muttering, "Baby steps, baby steps, baby steps." Although it was a silly movie, there was also some truth in it, truth that can assist us in getting past what we'll never get over.

Baby steps don't seem like much. They often go unnoticed or are blocked by the enormity of our struggles. Yet each seemingly insignificant step gives us confidence to take another, and then another.

It is often only in hindsight that we can look back and see, perhaps even celebrate, how far we've come. Too many times I am desperately searching for the big answer that will solve all my problems. Sometimes my stubbornness leads me to dig in and refuse to even consider small steps because they aren't enough of a solution. It usually takes a wise friend to point out that everything worth doing begins with small, seemingly insignificant steps.

The ability to recognize and affirm small steps in ourselves and in others is a sign that we are beginning to heal. Whether we are rehabbing our broken body or rehabbing our broken spirit, there usually is a decisive point when we take a first step forward.

We need other people's encouragement because we don't have perspective. Only time and experience give us perspective. I don't need people who have completely figured things out; I only need them to be a day ahead of me on the journey. Then I don't feel so alone and helpless.

Groups like Alcoholics Anonymous, Divorce Recovery, Employment Networks, and Grief Support can be effective because they invite people to share the journey toward wholeness. There is strength in growing together not only in spite of our great problems but even because of our problems. Burdens shared become lighter. Walking together through life's darkest times allows people to discover that their life is more significant than this present overshadowing difficulty, and they are esteemed and valued for who they are, not judged solely for what happened to them.

The ability to recognize and affirm small steps in ourselves and in others is a sign that we are beginning to heal.

Getting past what we'll never get over starts with small steps. When my wife Eileen struggled with agoraphobia, she became overwhelmed by panic attacks and couldn't stand to be in a crowd. She might suddenly jump up and run out of church or a restaurant, or refuse to enter a theater, believing that she would die from the suffocating panic.

Her world grew smaller and smaller. She quit her job, pulled away from friends, and turned down invitations to parties, all the while feeling shame because she wasn't like everyone else. Her therapist tried to encourage her by reminding her that she wouldn't always feel this way. Still, it was hard for her to believe him.

I remember the day we stepped from her apartment and slowly walked down the sidewalk to the corner mailbox. There she mailed a letter, and the two of us sat down on the curb next to the blue box to rest. As we sat there in the late afternoon sun, we promised to remember that moment. It was the first of many steps that led her up and out of her debilitating illness into a life of meaning and hope.

Was it a big, huge, miraculous step? Not to most people who drove past us that day. But to us, that baby step was gigantic. We'll never forget it.

3

The Myth of Normal

The only normal people are the ones you don't know very well.

Alfred Adler

I wanted to be normal. I wanted a normal family, with normal interests. I longed to fit in to what I thought normal people liked. It didn't happen. I was usually a few degrees off the plumb line. Sometimes I'd get down on myself for not fitting in, or seeming different, or perhaps even acting a little strange. I couldn't help it. My mind just didn't seem to work the way everyone else's mind worked.

I didn't process information in the normal way. I wasn't linear in my thoughts, nor was I a concrete/sequential thinker. I could come up with the correct answers in school and later in work situations, but I rarely could show the steps to how I got to that answer. It just seemed right to me. My mind would jump from A over to E without going through B, C, or D.

One of the recurring themes of my growing up years was, "Johnny has trouble with his mouth." And that was so true. I'd say things that didn't make sense to others, but in my odd way of looking at the world, were completely rational to me. Tasks that normal people accomplished in little time would require enormous amounts of effort from me just to get mediocre results. Obviously there was something "not right" with me. My efforts to fit in were mostly ineffective. It was only years later, as an adult, that I was diagnosed with attention deficit/hyperactivity disorder (ADHD).

Sometimes I wondered if I had character flaws that kept me from a normal life, or perhaps I had deep psychological problems. The pastor at the church I attended was convinced I was spiritually off base, and he would remind me that God couldn't use someone like me. I would have to become a completely different kind of person in order to fit into his good graces.

I tried to appear acceptable, but that only led to cultivating a false persona in order to fit in. It wasn't who I truly was as a person, and I learned that I was a fairly bad actor as well. Playing parts to please people was a losing option for me. In time, I realized that everywhere I went I found people who were pretending to be something or another. They were speaking and acting in ways that they thought would gain approval, but below the surface there was frustration over the dishonesty of their lives.

Who Decides Normal?

One of the difficulties with identifying "normal" lies in the cultural and social differences of society. What may be normal for one group of people may seem strange and odd to another. Years ago when actor Clint Eastwood ran in the election to become mayor of Carmel-by-the-Sea, an elite town in California, one of his campaign issues was to repeal the law forbidding ice cream cone consumption within the city limits. Campaign posters went up showing Clint holding an ice cream cone like a gun with the words, "Make my day!" Now, when you visit Carmel-by-the-Sea, you can actually see people eating ice cream cones while they walk through town. It's hard to believe this would have been an abnormal sight just a few years ago.

We've all seen people from other countries who are behaving in ways that would be normal in their homeland but appear bizarre to us. Surely some of the everyday habits of our normal life might appear strange or abnormal to someone from a different culture.

This can be anticipated and even expected when we are dealing with people from other countries or ethnic groups. However, there are many more subcultures operating that have their own understanding of what is normal. Organizations have norms for appropriate behavior or dress or even protocols for problem solving. Schools, churches, small towns, even families exert pressure to fit in and be normal. Even sick and twisted families have their yardstick for what is normal.

All the years we lived in Walnut Creek, California, we were unaware that about ten miles away in the town of Antioch, an eleven-year-old girl had been kidnapped and held prisoner by a sexual predator and his wife to be used as a sex slave. In her book *A Stolen Life* Jaycee Dugard describes herself before the kidnapping as a normal kid who did normal things. She had friends and a mother who loved her. She was just like us, until the day her life was stolen. For eighteen years she was a prisoner, an object for a monster to use and abuse. For eighteen years she was not allowed to speak her own name, though she became a mother at age fourteen and again when she was sixteen. Jaycee writes,

> I hated what he was doing to me, but I felt helpless to do anything about it. . . . I wanted to yell and scream to please let me go. He took me away from my family. From a mother that I loved with all my soul and I still needed desperately. He did disgusting things to me. In his mind he wanted us to be a family, but when I think back I can see we were just pretending. Pretending everything was okay. Pretending the girls didn't need to go to school. Pretending that it was normal for me not to be driving. Normal for us to not have friends. Normal that Phillip [her captor] was hearing voices.[1]

Our perceptions of what is normal are in constant flux. These changes occur because of emerging generations' influence of broadcast media, films, music, art, social media, and technology. Resentments increase as new "norms" are established and keepers of the old way feel their influence is diminishing.

Events such as the arrival of a new boss can result in great turmoil because the office culture will experience changes that result in new definitions of normal. Accepted procedures are suddenly challenged, established goals are reevaluated and altered, and channels of communication and decision-making processes are reinvented. This can be unsettling for people who liked the old ways. Their willingness to adapt to new ways of operating will either help establish the new normal or undermine the success of the organization and limit the ability of the new leader to institute change.

When Two Cultures Collide

What is normal for one person or group may not be normal for another. Because of our unique experiences, upbringing, training, and environments, the door is always open to misunderstanding and frustration. When we assume that others will enjoy something just because we do, we are met with disappointment and sometimes resentment.

My wife Eileen and I were invited to dinner at the home of friends who had recently come to the United States from their home in Malaysia. I was looking forward to the evening because I liked the people and I wanted to dine on a really authentic Asian meal. But things got complicated before we even reached our friends' home. When it came to eating, Eileen and I were already cross-cultural, and held on to very different ideas of what normal food should be. Now our differences were going to be tested by hosts who wanted to share the normal food of their homeland with us.

Of course, in my opinion Eileen is not an adventurous eater. The Irish American home she grew up in practiced the belief that boiling various foods until they lost their texture and flavor was the best (and only) cooking option. She also preferred bland flavors, to the extent that a little salt and pepper was considered highly seasoned. I, on the other hand, was a "hot head," priding myself on my ability to eat fiery and exotic foods as if they were a personal challenge to my manhood.

But despite this, things began well, I think. Eileen passed up much of the food she couldn't identify by pleading her case of being vegetarian. I worked my way through a bountiful feast including shark fin soup and many indiscernible morsels.

The crowning glory of the meal was the platter of freshly fried chicken feet. I was up for the challenge even though I was unnerved by the fact that there was no concealing this delicacy—it looked just like a plate of chicken feet.

Eileen turned her head away and pretended to be talking with the person beside her so as to not look at me putting feet in my mouth. I feigned enthusiasm and began to eat these "tasty" treats. First of all, when you eat chicken feet, prepare yourself for the fact that they aren't very meaty, but rather are an abundance of tiny bones. I nibbled and chewed and smiled my way through the platter while our hostess gazed with approval at my progress. When I finally fought my way through the serving, she jumped to her feet to bring out one more plateful, "Just because I enjoyed it so much."

Driving home, my wife and I had an energetic discussion about what is normal. I think we need more cross-cultural experiences in our life in order to challenge us to look beyond our comfort zone of normal living. Our tolerance for differences increases with every experience of someone else's normal life.

Getting Out of Routine

It is too easy to get used to a way of living, speaking, eating, or relating that is predictable and boring. In time we start to think that everyone ought to be just like us and what we consider normal should be normal for all people. For this reason I think it is helpful and perhaps even necessary to get out of our comfort zones and spend some time with people who are not like us. To that end, one year I took a sabbatical: three months for rest, study, reflection, and personal growth.

What could I do with three months of time away from work as well as my usual routines, recreations, and relationships? I had no idea how to spend the time in a meaningful way. I knew I should study, write, rest, renew, and spiritually revive. I knew I was genetically incapable of submitting to something as structured as a program at a university or seminary. I would have to make this one up on my own.

Tim, a colleague who had lived many years in Latin America, thought he had the best option for me. He made a few calls and persuaded someone to give me the use of a remote cabin in beautiful Brazil. How exotic did that sound? As he began to describe it for me, I could picture it in my mind: a beautiful lakefront setting deep in the woods, in a remote part of the country, several hours from the nearest city. It sounded like a dream.

It is too easy to get used to a way of living, speaking, eating, or relating that is predictable and boring.

The only problem was that for me, this dream might turn into a nightmare. You see, I am afraid of the dark, and unfamiliar, remote dark places scare the stew out of me.

Tim's offer took me back to an experience I had a few years ago. Some friends had offered me the use of their fabulous cabin up on a river in the mountains east of Seattle, so I could get away for a few days to study. I had jumped at the chance, packed my bags, and drove off toward the mountains for some quality alone time. Leaving the highway, I followed their directions and wound my way back into the woods. The cabins got farther apart as the road turned into a big trail, which soon became a small, barely discernible path. Finding the rusted old gate, I swung it open and proceeded up the gravel way to the remote vacation home.

Inside, I could tell it had been a place of happy memories. Pictures of normal parents and their two normal boys through the years were displayed with normal loving pride. Some showed them in winter ski gear, some in summer fishing apparel. I unpacked, set out my books and writing materials, and was all ready to allow myself to blend into this normal place. Dinner was easy to fix, and not long after, the evening shadows began to spread across the forest.

I think it was about 10:15 that evening when I thought I heard something by the side of the house. At least I think it was something—or maybe not. I would have gone outside to check, if it weren't for the fact that it seemed better to be devoured by a creature I didn't see than some horrifying monster that popped up in front of my face. Even as a little kid, I would never open my eyes when I thought there was a monster in my room, because if I couldn't see it there was a good chance it might not see me. Perhaps this is how denial plants its stubborn seed into our fragile little minds.

But I was not a little kid. I was a respected, overly educated, mature adult on a little study getaway. So I did what I thought was the reasonable thing to do under the circumstances: I grabbed my stuff, jumped into the car, and drove home as fast as the old car could carry me.

So that remote cabin deep in the woods of Brazil wasn't going to work for me. Tim took the news pretty well, but he didn't give up trying to help me have a great learning experience. In fact, his whole family got into the game of "find John a place to go." His aunt won the prize. She found a small farm in Bavaria that I could rent, and the best part was it was located in a small village consisting of a cluster of small family farms. I wouldn't be alone, and there was a quaint town only a few kilometers away. Who could ask for anything more?

My plans fell together smoothly and effortlessly. I'd fly to Munich, rent a car, and drive to the city of Passau. From there I would drive up into the countryside toward the Czech border, where I would make myself at home and unleash the creative side of my brain. Language would of course not be a problem for me, since I had one year of high school German under my belt. But just to be on the safe side, I bought a "Learn German" computer program at Costco that I was confident would have me speaking like a native in a few days. After all, it even included a microphone so I could see a little meter on the screen that let me know how my accent and pronunciation were improving.

Everything was going according to plan. I flew to Munich and rented a car, and drove through the beautiful country-side until I reached Passau. This city is significant for its three rivers converging right in the center of town. I'd read that Napoleon occupied the place for a while as he planned the expansion of his empire. So far, I was in the right place. Then I reached the spot where my directions indicated I should turn left. However, there on the corner was a sign with my destination town's name and an arrow pointing to the right. So off to the right I went, toward Austria, feeling a little like Clark Griswold in *European Vacation*. Several hours later, as evening was approaching, I arrived in a town but it didn't seem to have any of the landmarks that were so carefully described in my directions. After driving around in a dazed and confused state of mind, I stopped by some pedestrians to ask for help. Right then the limit of my language skills began to emerge. Each local citizen invited friends into the discussion—which had no discernible meaning to me. Finally it was determined that I wanted the town with the same name in Germany—and this was the town in Austria. They gazed in wonder at me as they tried to figure out how I had arrived in the wrong country. So I spent my evening driving back the way I had come, returning to my notorious "intersection of doom." There, under some low-lying tree branches, was the sign telling me to indeed turn left if I wanted to remain in Germany. The rest of my journey went without mishap, and at last I arrived at the farm.

The little farmhouse and barn were quaint in a rural European way. I soon set up my life and began to acclimate to my surroundings. I spent a few hours each morning working on my language skills, since it became apparent that if, in fact, anyone in the locale could understand English, they certainly weren't going to let it show. The adventurous part of each day was my journey into town where I pretended to be a normal person, buying normal supplies such as cheese, bread, and assorted necessities containing large amounts of chocolate.

My normal encounters with the local folks usually went something like this: I would stand at the counter waiting my turn to order while my mind raced to find the right words to appear normal. Then I would greet the clerk with my friendliest, well-accented conversational German, which sounded to me like the commands of the *Das Boot* submarine captain. After a brief greeting, the clerk usually swamped me with very fast foreign words that left me standing in a stunned stupor. After many struggles and gestures, I was able to order my little piece of cheese and a sausage, though I was never sure if I would in fact receive the items ordered. It didn't really matter, because surrender and escape were foremost in my mind. Finally, the transaction would be completed, and usually by this time the other store clerks had gathered around to play "guess what the foreign guy is saying." I often walked out exhausted and humiliated.

Just knowing that the next day I would have to go through it all over again motivated me to keep studying the Costco program. Although the clerks were always smiling and kind, I got the sense that when I left the shop they'd turn to each other and say, "He seems like such a nice, friendly man; he must be a burden to his poor family. Imagine not being smart enough to answer the simplest questions."

A few doors down from the cheese shop was the town's little bakery. Every day I'd stop by to smell the air and buy an assortment of bread, rolls, and pastries. Being without preservatives, the bread would get stale fairly fast, but that didn't faze me because I knew I'd be going in the next day to buy more. After about a week, the lady behind the counter stopped smiling and started glaring at me whenever I entered her shop. She seemed a little upset and worried about something. Being the kind, warm-hearted person that I am, I asked if everything was all right.

She began to share her frustration about my eating habits. In a halting combination of German, English, and hand signals, she tried to explain to me how the village normally worked. For years their little shop has made the bread, rolls, and pastries for the families around the town. They got used to the appetites of their neighbors, and baked just the right amount of each item so that the village was supplied with its bakery needs, and there was very little wasted.

However, she let me know that since I had come to town, with my wasteful overbuying and unpredictable selection of items, she had become quite frustrated. She gruffly pointed out that when I bought bread *and* rolls *and* pastries the shop would run out of items. Then, when one of the local townspeople came in for their regular purchase, there was nothing left for them.

Evidently she thought I was personally responsible for the decline and destruction of the entire food supply and economy of the village. What could I do? I certainly didn't want to disturb the delicate balance of a living environment that had functioned quite normally for hundreds of years.

That was when I learned what every German child understood by about age two. The bakery lady sternly explained to me that since I was living alone, I had no business buying a whole loaf of bread at all. Instead, I should ask for a *halb brot*, a "half loaf." In fact, she suggested that I just request the amount of bread I needed by indicating with my fingers, and she would happily cut just the right amount for me. In the same way I could buy only the number of rolls I would realistically eat in one day, then come in the next day and get more. Of course, from Saturday noon to Monday morning they were closed, so she would anticipate my buying a little more on Saturday morning to get me through the weekend.

That was the way I learned what was normal according to the customs of the Bavarian village, and the villagers were saved the ordeal of lighting torches and storming my little farmhouse, seeking the foreign monster who had devoured their last pastry.

Rethinking Heroes

I'm coming to realize that in life, as it is in the Bible, there are not too many authentic heroes. From time to time some folks appear perfectly heroic, but eventually they are shown to be all too human. One of these was Moses.

Ever since I saw *The Ten Commandments* at the drive-in movies when I was a kid, I was fascinated with Moses; particularly as portrayed by Charleton Heston. I thought of him as someone whom people would respect, admire, and see as a great hero and leader. I was only around nine years old, but I appreciated this wonderful person up on the screen who was committed in his relationship with God and was able to communicate God's message to the people. Who doesn't like Moses? I even went to see the cartoon version *Prince of Egypt* many years later.

Imagine my disappointment when I found out that my childhood hero worship was based on shaky assumptions. Paul writes in 2 Corinthians 3:13: "We are not like Moses, who would put a veil over his face to keep the Israelites from gazing at it while the radiance was fading away." When I read that, I couldn't help but think Moses pretended to be more holy by covering his face with a veil so people wouldn't see his fading glory and would keep thinking he was special. Why? Because Moses was human, just like us. I think Paul was challenging the tendency people have to elevate certain people to hero status by reminding them that Moses was not perfect.

Sure, he came away from God's presence with his face glowing so brightly that people had to turn away. The Bible relates in Exodus 34 that Moses put a veil over his face, covering the glow, to ease the discomfort of those who came to see him.

But what happened? In time the glow would fade, leaving Moses just a regular person once again. This wouldn't have been an issue, except that Moses must have liked being considered special. I know I would. Perhaps, not wanting anyone to know he was just a normal, regular guy, he continued to wear the veil long after it was no longer needed.

Maybe he didn't want to disappoint anyone, or he wanted to live up to others' expectations of what they wanted their leader to be. Whatever the reason, it may have been powerful enough to prompt Moses to lie to them by wearing a mask, pretending to be better than he was. Why was this story left out of the movie?

When we pretend to be something we are not, or pretend to be more than we are, or pretend so that others will think better of us, we undermine our chance to get past our pain and live effective lives. This is not a new phenomenon. All the way back in the Garden of Eden, we see that Adam and Eve hid themselves because they were afraid of being found out. We've spent our lives covering up and hiding because we too are scared of being found out.

Swiss psychiatrist Paul Tournier observed:

> The truth is that human beings are much more alike than they think. What is different is the external mask—sparkling or disagreeable. What is different is the outward reaction—in the strong or weak. These appearances, however, hide an identical inner personality. The external mask and the outward reaction deceive everybody—the strong as well as the weak. All, in fact, are weak. All are weak because all are afraid. They are afraid of being trampled underfoot. They are afraid of their inner weakness being discovered. We all have secret faults. We all have a bad conscience on account of certain acts which

46

we would like to keep covered up. We are all afraid of others and of God, of ourselves, of life and of death.[2]

Peer pressure can encourage us to appear good, righteous, and strong, and we cover up our flaws so people won't see how weak we really are. But there is also a flipside. When it is not fashionable to be righteous, people can pretend to be scoundrels in order to appear normal to the people they wish to impress.

I'm coming to believe our self-esteem is not based on what we think of ourselves, nor is it based on what other people think of us. Rather, it is based on what we think others think of us. This leads us to continually search the eyes of people around us, hoping to determine what they want or need from us. Then we attempt to please, hoping to appear normal, and perhaps make us feel better about ourselves.

As a teenager I played guitar in a few bands and musical groups. One night I was in a group performing in Los Angeles when the director called me up to the microphone. Turned out he wanted to have a druggy, hippie testimony that night. So he selected me because of appearances: I was playing the guitar and had long hair. Looking out at the audience, he said, "Now John, you came to follow Jesus, leaving behind a wild life of drugs. Then didn't you write this next song coming out of a drug-induced haze? Jesus met you and saved you from that. Isn't that right?"

What was I going to say? "No! I'm a Christian—I didn't do that. I may own and operate a psychedelic shop called the Joint Effort, but I don't do drugs." That would have been the truth, but instead I said what he wanted me to say. "Oh, yeah, that's right."

At the time, I was dating a pretty blonde girl named Eileen and I wanted to impress her. She had come to the concert and was sitting in the audience. I saw a look flash over her face that gave the message, *I don't know this man. He told me he never did drugs, and now I am hearing this story in front of hundreds of people about how God saved him from a life of drug addiction. Who is he, really?* It's amazing how much can be communicated in one brief glance. She was so mad she didn't talk to me for two weeks.

I wanted to fit in, so I just went along. I was a hypocrite. I pretended to be worse than I was. As Oscar Wilde wrote in *The Importance of Being Earnest,* "I hope you have not been leading a double life. Pretending to be wicked and being really good all the time. That would be hypocrisy."[3]

Pretending to be better or worse than we are can be an expression of hypocrisy. Deep inside we all know we are fragile and easily broken. But we are afraid that if the image cracks a little bit, if the mask we wear to cover up our true feelings gives way, we won't be able to fulfill other people's expectations.

I was in a small group for years. Finally one of the people in the group told me, "We don't mind you always telling stories of failure and stories of pain week after week. We don't mind it because we love you, but something good has got to have happened in your life sometime that you could share with us." I realized I wasn't comfortable sharing the good things, so I kept on the mask of struggle when actually I was doing some pretty great things in my life. Not being comfortable with success, I kept up the façade of struggle. And like my old hero Moses, I kept wearing the mask so everything would appear normal.

Things Are Not Always as They Appear

Years ago in Los Angeles, an exciting story was reported in the news. I was amazed to hear how a homeless man, struggling to live, came upon a child who had disappeared from an arcade while his mom was distracted. The child had been missing for several days. The man found the little boy, took care of him, and brought him to the police station to be returned to his anguished family. The man was heralded as an instant hero. Everyone joyfully celebrated, and he gained fame through television interviews and exuberant media attention. A financial reward was presented from a local business association, and job offers poured in to help him rebuild his broken life.

A few weeks later a second miracle occurred. Another missing child was found by the same man and brought to the police station. As before, the family rejoiced, the media reported the story, and I wondered what the chances were of this happening twice in such a short time.

Some time later, I noticed a tiny article buried in the back pages of our newspaper. It mentioned how that homeless man had been sentenced to eight years in prison for kidnapping those two boys.

I think he just wanted to appear normal. He didn't want to be homeless, nor did he want to live on the frayed edge of society. Perhaps, when he saw the child separated from his mother, he envisioned a way out of his problems. I can understand the pressure to make ourselves look good and appear normal in the eyes of other people. Unfortunately, when the truth comes out we are often exposed as the phonies we have become.

Depending on our background and experiences, our perspectives about what is normal will vary greatly. I've found myself in situations where I made assumptions about what was happening, but I was very wrong. Not every beautiful landscape is a peaceful, trouble-free experience. Looking out over the Puget Sound from our front window, I am captivated by the beauty and the apparent peacefulness of the water. However, from a distance it is impossible to recognize all the potential threats and problems just below the calm surface. Just because someplace looks beautiful and idyllic doesn't mean it is safe.

While in Zambia exploring ministry partnerships to help AIDS orphans, we were invited to detour a couple of days for a safari experience. Because I had not been back to Africa since living there as a child, I eagerly signed up. Leaving our encampment at dawn, we crossed a great river while watching the sun rise over the water. Then we bumped along in an old truck for a couple of hours while our guides pointed out wildlife and helped us spot things like monkeys in the trees or a herd of elephants in the distance.

Midway through the experience we stopped at a remote watering hole where we could get out of the truck and stretch our legs while snacking on tea and cookies. I ambled off by myself to the water's edge some distance from the truck and enjoyed the stillness and beauty of this rare "African" moment.

Suddenly I heard a commotion from the vicinity of the truck, and turned to see a guide waving his arms and yelling at me to get away from the water. I waved back to let him know that I was fine and he didn't need to concern himself with me. All at once he ran to me and grabbed me, pulling me back from the edge of the lake. *What a nutcase*, I thought. *What is the big deal anyway?*

That's when he pointed out the barely visible protrusions of two big crocodiles that had evidently quietly been approaching the spot where I had been standing only a minute ago. Then, as if to emphasize that I was an idiot, he pointed to the hulking forms of hippos near the water's edge. Evidently they are even more dangerous than the crocs. While all this was sinking in, he then pointed out a huge mass floating in the lake and told me it was the carcass of a hippo that had lost a fight with the others. He of course also mentioned that below the surface the crocs had been devouring its flesh . . . and then I didn't want another cookie. I began to consider that not everything is how it appears to be. Not all beauty is peaceful, and not all animals are meant to be cuddled.

Riding back to our safari camp, we talked about the experiences of the day and admitted feeling disappointment that we didn't have an opportunity to be "up close and personal" with any wild animals. As we climbed the path from the river's edge toward the lodge, we heard loud thrashing sounds coming from nearby overgrowth not far from the water's edge. Approaching a bend in the trail, we suddenly found ourselves face-to-face with a huge bull elephant ambling toward us.

Earlier that morning we had seen a group of elephants in the distance and they appeared much smaller from that perspective. This one was big and getting closer. Some of our teammates grabbed their cameras and began taking pictures of the elephant. Jerry, a member of the team, wanted a special picture as a souvenir. Dressed in his stylish "safari outfit" he had bought at REI (a purveyor of outdoor and safari-like apparel), he began advancing on the elephant, calling to the others to take a picture of him standing next to the huge beast.

Suddenly a woman came running in our direction from the lodge. She was shouting and gesturing to get away from the elephant immediately. To my thinking she was being quite rude and pushy, especially since she didn't know us nor was she even an employee at the lodge. Jerry kept getting closer and closer to the elephant in spite of the woman's warnings and apparently irrational bossiness. Finally she grabbed him by the arm and roughly yanked him away from the seemingly docile elephant.

I didn't appreciate her rudeness or her self-appointed role as rule keeper. So I went immediately to report her to the manager of the lodge. After I complained to the manager about our uncomfortable encounter with the hostile guest, she leaned back in her chair and informed me that two weeks ago that same elephant had come up the path from the river. Evidently there were several of that lady's friends who had run down to take pictures. The elephant had suddenly attacked one of the tourists and stomped him to death right in front of this woman. With a shrug, the manager suggested that perhaps she had been adamant because she didn't want to witness another tourist being killed.

As I left the office I felt stupid, but I was also impressed by the manager's apparent nonchalance. Perhaps she just assumed there would be consequences for getting too close to wild animals—otherwise why would we refer to them as wild? Maybe I needed to rethink my assumptions about our world. Just getting away or getting back to nature won't necessarily result in peace. What is normal in one setting may not be normal in another.

How can we experience peace in the midst of the potential dangers all around us? Can we appreciate beauty while being wise about what we can't see? After Zambia, I think peace may be less about quiet alone time and more about becoming our authentic, true selves in this beautiful and dangerous world.

When Real Becomes Normal

In his book *Ruthless Trust*, Brennan Manning writes:

> The great weakness in the North American church at large and certainly in my own life is our refusal to accept our brokenness. We hide it, evade it, and gloss over it. We grab for the cosmetic kit and put on our virtuous face to make ourselves admirable to the public. Thus we present to others a self that looks spiritually together, superficially happy and lacquered with a sense of self-deprecating humor that passes for humility. The irony is that while I do not want anyone to know that I am judgmental, lazy, vulnerable, screwed up and afraid, for fear of losing face, the face that I fear losing is the mask of the imposter, not my own.[4]

While we may appear quite different on the surface, we actually have much in common. Thus we don't have to pretend. We can be transparent. The danger of living hypocritically is that, in time, we come to believe the lies. We start to believe them because they slowly become part of our persona.

We can change and discover life beyond our masks. The experience will be different for each of us, but we can all be

Isn't it time to stop leading double lives and choose to be authentic, transparent men and women?

53

free to be the people God had in mind when he first thought of us. Isn't it time to stop leading double lives and choose to be authentic, transparent men and women? Imagine a world where it is normal to be real. Where we laugh and love and work and dream without fear of being found out, because we have nothing to hide.

One of the most important steps we can take to get past what we'll never get over is the one that brings us out of hiding, pretending, and covering up. It might feel a little strange at first, but in time we will feel normal.

4

The Joy of Depression

Depression is the inability to construct a future.

Rollo May

If there is one thing I know about, it is depression. There's been no time in my life when I wouldn't have described myself as being depressed. Much of the time it was a low-grade, shadowy depression that followed me around like the dust swirling behind Charlie Brown's friend Pigpen in the *Peanuts* cartoons. This surprises many of the people who know me, because my inner experience of depression had little to do with the persona I presented to the world.

Millions of people are diagnosed with a form of clinical depression. There are millions more who suffer although they are not yet diagnosed. People who experience depression are often misunderstood. Meeting with family and friends of those who are depressed has shown me how easy it is to dismiss the problem and blame the person experiencing the pain. "They are lazy. Why don't they try harder? What is the matter with them?" Judgment comes in many forms; it can be overt and abrasive, but it can also be subtle and quietly insulting. Unfortunately a depressed person may not "need" the condemnation of others—because there is plenty of inner condemnation taking place. There may be no greater accuser than the one who is experiencing the depression.

Depression can touch anyone. Stress or trauma affecting brain chemistry can bring on bouts of debilitating depression. It can become a mood disorder that slowly diminishes confidence and destroys lives. It can wreck health and well-being, diminish self-esteem, and undermine relationships. Untreated, it can carry the sufferer to the brink of self-destruction. Long considered primarily a women's malady (perhaps due to mis diagnosis by Sigmund Freud), it is now known to affect people across life's spectrum.

Jimmy Brown, a New York City firefighter, ran for his life down the stairs of the World Trade Center on 9/11. He barely got out alive, but he paid a price. He took up smoking again, and began to drink too much. He felt paralyzed by an overwhelming sense of sadness and anxiety. He said, "I started to feel like I had absolutely no purpose in life. I'd get up in the morning and wonder what I was getting up for." When he finally went for medical help, the diagnosis was depression.[1]

Low energy levels, prevailing tiredness, and feelings of hopelessness are all common experiences with depression. Often depression joins with other problems to create an even more difficult condition. Sometimes anxiety links up with depression to create panic attacks and edgy restlessness. Unresolved anger and resentments can fester alongside depression.

When I took my son Damian to the doctor to be tested for ADHD, I was asked to participate in one section of the testing to give a family member's perspective. It wasn't very long into the interview when the physician suddenly turned to me and said, "It won't take a three-hour test to determine that you could be the poster child for adult ADHD." That observation led me to look back on much of my life and the range of emotional experiences I had undergone. I learned that those of us with ADHD commonly experience bouts of depression that increase the difficulty of completing tasks and accomplishing goals. A prevailing sense of hopelessness can lead a person to focus on events that are tragic, debilitating, and irrational, thus providing "reasons" to justify the pain we are experiencing. This in turn fosters the recurring torment of regret.

In a way, depression can be equal to and sometimes even more difficult than other painful maladies, simply because when a person has a physical ailment they are often affirmed, loved, and encouraged with hope and self-esteem. When a person breaks their arm, for example, they might receive cards and notes of encouragement, people will commit to pray for them, and often there is joyful celebration over signs of recovery. Not so with depression. It is not uncommon for friends and even family to pull away from someone suffering with depression. There are no cards or bright flower arrangements, nor is there appreciation and encouragement for small steps of improvement. The depressed person can find the accompanying isolation and loneliness to be more painful than the original disease.

Fortunately, depression can be readily treated. Yet many people go through their lives undiagnosed, feeling that they have a character flaw or are a bad person. The ramifications can be startling. American businesses reportedly lose $44 billion a year because of workplace depression. While half of that loss is because of absenteeism, the other half is because of employees who, like zombies in low-budget movies, are there in body but not in spirit. And while depressed women might consider a variety of treatments, men who are depressed are more prone to choose suicide as the only way out.[2]

Depression is simply not understood by most people. Unless we or someone close to us suffers with it, we have very little experience to draw on in order to relate in helpful and positive ways. Even mental health professionals often disagree about causes, treatments, and best practices for those suffering from depression. Our tendency with most problems is to expect instant results, quick answers, and speedy solutions. The greater our pain, the less tolerant we become of long treatment processes.

Although there may be reasons or specific incidents in a person's life that might be seen to explain the depression, depression is not always linked to events or experiences at all. Chemical reactions within our nervous systems affect us in a multitude of ways. Thus life can seem bleak and hopeless for no discernible reason.

Even in my growing up years, when life turned my way and things were going well, I still wasn't happy. Education, marriage, fatherhood, career, travel, books, conference speaking, radio programs, country clubs, lots of good friends . . . even a growing faith and deepening commitment to Jesus Christ didn't stem the tide of my depression.

While being interviewed by *Rolling Stone* magazine on the occasion of his fiftieth birthday, Bob Dylan was asked if he was happy. After sitting in silence for a few moments, staring down at his hands, he replied, "You know those are yuppie words, happiness and unhappiness. It's not happy or unhappy—it's either blessed or unblessed."[3] It made sense to me that we could be considering ourselves blessed, rather than happy with all its superficial overtones. I was relieved to have him point that out. I think my lack of happiness made me feel a bit like an outsider in a world where people can feel pressure to act happy even if it isn't what they are experiencing. After all, we live in a country founded on the principle that everyone is entitled to "life, liberty, and the pursuit of happiness." Perhaps this underlying creed has lured us into our current obsession with pursuing and achieving happiness. Our attempts to do so may have hurt us in the long run, because we can miss experiencing real joy.

I once read a quote from actress Parker Posey that resonated with me. She said, "I can do comedy, so people want me to do that, but the other side of comedy is depression. Deep, deep depression is the flipside of comedy. Casting agents don't realize it but in order to be funny you have to have that other side."[4]

Her insight rang true for me. I too could be funny, perhaps even irritatingly funny. The class clown, the outrageous outspoken guy who always had a quick, funny retort for any situation—that was me. I didn't see depression and humor as mutually exclusive. In reality they both lived quite comfortably inside me.

On some level, I also believed creativity and passion were linked to the ache and angst of my feelings of depression. I wondered what kind of person I might have been without the depression affecting my mind and body. I realize now that for years I wasn't committed to getting past the sadness, tiredness, loneliness, negativity, and hopelessness of the depression because I was afraid I might lose something that made me uniquely me. I didn't want to turn into an average, predictable person. After all, the world was filled with folks like that. I wanted to be different.

When depression is the air we breathe, it creates its own familiarity and connectedness with our life. Eventually we can become comfortable with its presence. We get used to feeling a certain way and no longer question whether what we are feeling is appropriate or healthy. Depression fades into the fabric of our life. It is still present; we are merely oblivious to it. Sometimes we get so comfortable with it that we are afraid of losing it. Looking back, it seems a little crazy that I was hesitant to give up my depression. But much of the time it didn't bother me that much. I just assumed it was the way everyone felt. Besides, as long as it stayed in the background, like emotional wallpaper, I felt free to identify with people's personal issues and to share and care with vulnerability and genuine concern. But it was affecting me in ways I didn't even realize.

I was growing increasingly sullen and negative when I was away from other people. Unfortunately, I used up most of my energy with other people and didn't have much left to give to my family. One day I overheard a woman talking with my wife. "Your husband is so funny," she said. "You must have so much fun and laughter in your home, being married to him." Eileen flinched a little and responded (a bit too quickly I think), "No, no, he may be fun out with others, but at home he usually mopes around like a giant couch potato."

It hurt to hear her say that, but I knew it was true. So I began to look for signs that my depression was affecting my behavior. I didn't have to look far. I found that I would shoot down new ideas without giving them fair consideration; I also noticed I was pulling away from social settings and seeking more time to be alone. Always gregarious and extroverted, I now noticed that I was feeling depleted by interactions with people, where before I had come away from those encounters energized. Worst of all, I came to see that I didn't like the person I was becoming.

One evening, I overheard our son talking with Eileen. Damian said, "I wish Dad would be the Rev at home sometimes." I knew what he was talking about. Around town I was called "The Rev," because I was energetic and fun and creative. Even the license plate on my sports car had "The Rev" on it. But with my own family I was no fun to be with. Something in me needed to change.

Change Will Come

Change comes at unexpected moments. Even though I didn't see my changes coming, reality was about to break into my world in a radical way. It began on a Sunday morning in January; I was feeling pretty good, for me. I had just preached our 9:00 worship service and felt satisfied. The service was well attended that morning, with over eight hundred people packed into our sanctuary. Afterward I made my way to the church gym where folks gathered for donuts and conversation. It was a fun time meeting visitors and greeting longtime members; the coffee was strong and the donuts were sweet.

After a while, I checked my watch and saw I still had time to get home to watch the early football playoff game, so I headed out to the parking lot. As I was unlocking my car, I noticed one of our elders making a beeline across the parking lot toward me. I greeted him and asked how things were going with his family and work. I was fishing around to see if there was a problem or concern he wanted to share with me. He kept looking at me in a questioning way, and then he blurted out, "There are hundreds of people waiting in the sanctuary without a pastor." I stood there for a moment—and then it hit me. *We have a second service, don't we?* Together we sprinted back to the sanctuary.

I slipped in, sat down, and tried to get my bearings. *How could I forget we have a second service? What is wrong with me?* I stumbled through the service and preached the sermon through a haze of preoccupation. Of course that was the worship service my wife attended.

"What happened to you?" she blurted out the minute we got home. "I figured something was really wrong, because you are so careful about time on Sundays. You would never miss a worship service. I assumed some disgruntled member had shot you on the patio." I nervously laughed it off, but she was adamant. "Maybe you are getting Alzheimer's and are losing your memory. Something is not right."

Though I tried to minimize it and explain it away, I too wondered how this could have happened. So at Eileen's insistence, the next day I called a psychiatrist and made an appointment for him to check me out.

Walking into his office for the first time was both frightening and exciting. Yes, I was afraid of what might be found below the surface of my mind and personality. At the same time I was excited in the way one might feel starting out on a trip to a foreign land.

At the end of the evaluation, the doctor sat back in his overstuffed chair and said, "I'm not a neurologist, so I can't say with absolute certainty that you do not have Alzheimer's, but I don't believe that is your problem." He paused for a second, and added, "But you are in a very deep depression." He then presented me with a choice. Either I worked through the depression with a combination of medication and psychotherapy, or, he said, "Tell the church you are cutting back to only one service on Sunday. Because your body is telling you that is all you can do right now."

I was relieved that our worst fears weren't coming true, yet I realized I had been found out as being somewhat less than an all-powerful, vigilant, pastoral Superman. Could something as basic as depression really have the power to short-circuit my brain and undermine my effectiveness in ministry? That day I made a commitment to rise above my depression and attempt to experience life as it was meant to be lived.

We tried different antidepressant medications until we landed on one that seemed to work without adverse side effects. I jumped into therapy with a determination to break the grip of whatever was sabotaging me. My doctor explored with me most aspects of my life, working on predictable pathologies and some issues I wasn't even aware of. We talked about my early childhood experiences and unresolved issues within my family of origin. I processed, journaled, did homework, interviewed, cogitated, discussed, and prayed through the remaining winter and on into spring.

I clearly remember the Tuesday afternoon in late May when I sat down in the psychiatrist's office. He asked me how I was feeling. "Well, I'm not depressed," I said. In that moment I realized that this was the first time in my life I had uttered those words. Up until then I would have answered, "Well, I'm depressed but . . ."

He smiled and asked how my life would be different now that I wasn't depressed. He then pushed further, asking what kind of man I would be now that I wasn't depressed. I was stumped. I thought for a while and then told him that I didn't know, having had no experience of this before. He laughed and told me I should go out and live, letting myself experience life without the shadows of depression clouding up my mind and emotions. "Go find out what kind of person you are now," he said. With that encouragement I walked out into my new life.

Just Like Us

In James 5:17, we read that Elijah was a person just like us. He had great faith and saw his prayers answered in tangible, miraculous ways, yet he became deeply depressed. I am intrigued by Elijah because his life had incredible highs and cavernous lows, as well as long periods of just sitting around. The incident that gives us a description of his depression, as well as showing how the Lord dealt with him, occurs in 1 Kings 18 and 19. Elijah is coming off what may have been the greatest victory of his life. He has miraculously tested God's power and humiliated King Ahab's priests. Then he took things a step further by killing all the prophets of Baal. Jezebel, Ahab's wife, was furious and threatened to murder Elijah in retaliation for his actions.

When Elijah learns of the plot to take his life, he flees, running as far and as fast as he can to get away from the fate awaiting him. The Bible tells us that he basically ran himself into exhaustion and then sank into a suicidal depression.

One day he is running away to save his life, then when he is overwhelmed with depression, he prays for God to kill him or at least let him die.

James says Elijah was a person just like us and Scripture shows us that, like Elijah, we can experience huge victories and still fall into a state of depression that threatens to debilitate us. However, God does not leave Elijah alone in misery and exhaustion. Instead, he comes and interrupts his depression in very specific ways.

"There are many reasons for your depression," writes Greg Jantz, "but God's desiring you to be unhappy and miserable is not one of them. God is not your adversary in depression but your greatest and most powerful resource for recovery. He is totally on your side in this struggle."[5]

The prophet finally collapses in depression. He is exhausted, hungry, and alone, having left his servant behind on the road. The first divine interruption is the "messenger" who wakes Elijah two times to encourage him to eat. He tells him, "Get up and eat, for the journey is too much for you" (see 1 Kings 19:5–9). Nourishing sleep and nourishing food, then more sleep and more food, are required to give Elijah the strength to move on.

When experiencing depression, one of the first things to go is self-care. We don't take care of ourselves in a variety of ways. Personal health tends to be neglected and we stop eating, or we eat in ways that are harmful or self-destructive. When sleep patterns are interrupted, we easily lose touch with natural rhythms of healthy living.

Healthy eating, normal sleep patterns, and nurturing relationships team with appropriate medications and professional treatment to form a foundation on which our lives can remain whole and unencumbered by depression. Obviously this doesn't happen in an instant, but over time it is possible for us to live beyond our depression.

Elijah had evidently gone for several days without food or sleep. He also disconnected from his personal support system by leaving his servant behind and traveling on by himself. With no one in his life to come alongside supporting, encouraging, and helping, is it any surprise that the prophet collapsed in physical and emotional despair?

Michael Hunt, a psychiatrist in the UK, notes:

> Depression is like a thief in the night. It robs you of your life unless you're strong enough to seek help. Depression is usually best treated with a combination of medication and group or individual psychotherapy. With treatment people can come to realize that having depression does not mean having a character defect. What they often find is a greater appreciation of themselves and their lives.[6]

In addition to healthy eating and sleep patterns, supportive relationships are also important for us to handle the stress and strain of daily life. They are crucial in times of crisis, loss, and personal distress. Unfortunately, while experiencing great pain it is possible to send away the very people who could provide nurture, support, and encouragement.

Trying to cope on our own, we can lose perspective and become erratic in caring for ourselves. We begin to eat in order to feel comfort, only to find ourselves gaining weight and feeling sluggish and weak. Or, like Elijah, some people just stop eating. Their bodies, running on adrenaline, keep going for a while, so they assume everything is all right—until finally they collapse in exhaustion. Some people respond by sleeping all the time. With depression can come an overwhelming sense of exhaustion, making it difficult to get out of bed in the morning. No amount of sleep ever satisfies. We can lie in bed all day, or find ourselves falling asleep at irregular or inappropriate times such as while driving a car, while in a meeting, at our desk, or at a social gathering.

On the other hand, we may find it nearly impossible to sleep at all. Insomnia or restlessness through the night robs us of our needed sleep. We find ourselves dreading the night, because we can't sleep even though we are racked by tiredness. The torment of a sleep disorder can lead to self-medicating, whereby we try to fix ourselves with alcohol or drugs.

When Elijah collapsed in suicidal depression, he was not given advice nor was he told to simply get over it. Instead he was encouraged to sleep and eat, then sleep and eat some more. Only then was he in a healthy enough state of mind to deal with his unresolved issues. Our bodies need enough sleep to maintain our capacity for healing. Only then are we able to take meaningful steps toward healing our mind and body.

Supportive relationships are crucial to overcoming depression.

Supportive relationships are crucial to overcoming depression. Maintaining connections with people is not always easy, because we see ourselves as no fun to be around or as unworthy of friends. We can convince ourselves that since we have nothing valuable to offer in a relationship, no one would want to connect with us. So why bother even trying?

Elijah was instructed to go back the way he came, and as he went he met Elisha, a young man who would become his close friend and colleague. From that day onward, Elijah was no longer a loner living in self-imposed exile. He was now connecting and relating, and working side by side with others.

I know it may sound strange, but I am getting to a place in my life where I can appreciate having been a depressed person for so many years. I'm sometimes even thankful for the experience, because I no longer have a fear of depression, nor am I without hope when I share with fellow sufferers. I'm grateful for the healing I have come to know on the journey, and even find joy in realizing that I'm a stronger person for the experiences I went through.

5

It Can't Happen Here!

I don't need to manufacture trauma in my life to
be creative. I have a big enough reservoir of sadness or emotional trauma to last me.

Sting

It was going to be another warm day in Los Angeles. Already
the smog was beginning to throw its dull blanket across the
city. We had moved into an old house less than six weeks ago,
just before the start of my graduate classes. We had almost
finished the unpacking and organizing that are a large part
of making empty rooms feel like home.

On this August morning, I left for work at a restaurant
where I was a waiter during the busy lunch hour. Eileen was
determined to finish the little jobs that would finally settle
us into the new life we were beginning.

She was totally absorbed in her chores when she suddenly
looked up to find a man peering through the glass half of

the back door. "I'm looking for Pat, is she here?" he said in a cold, menacing voice.

With a creeping feeling of uneasiness, she said, "No, there's no one here by that name."

"Are you sure she's not here?" he asked again, suddenly pushing open the door as he moved toward her.

Before she could answer, he lunged at her and knocked her to the floor. Unleashing his rage, the stranger began screaming, "You're gonna die, do you hear me? I'm gonna kill you right here!"

"What do you want, who are you, why are you doing this to me?" Eileen cried. "I just moved here. . . . I'm not the one you're looking for!" He responded by grabbing a heavy antique soup ladle from the sink and beating her repeatedly across the head as he continued to scream, "You're gonna die!"

At first she struggled to break away, but as the blows crashed down on her head she began to feel weak and faint. Blood was flowing down her face and arms, soaking into her dress.

We all hear about violent crime from the newspaper and on television, but those events seem far removed from our own life. Perhaps we all view urban violence as something that happens to someone else. It can't happen in our town, in our neighborhood, on our street, or in our home. But now it was happening in our home. My wife was experiencing the horror of a nightmare, and began to pray she would not become another statistic on the evening news.

Pulling an ice pick from his jacket, the man pressed its deadly tip against her throat, then wrapped her bloodied hair around his fist and dragged her from room to room searching for money, weapons, and valuables. Her head was throbbing. "Please stop hurting me," she stammered. "Take anything in the house, but let me go! Please!"

"You're not going anywhere," he said angrily as he continued to drag her through the house. Once the telephone rang, interrupting the bizarre drama, but on the eighth ring the sound stopped. Once again Eileen felt totally alone, helpless, and in the hands of a murderer.

Finally he shoved her into the closet of a small bedroom. "Make one noise, and I'll give you this," he threatened, waving the point of the ice pick inches away from her eyes. "I have some things to do before I finish with you."

Alone in the dark space of the tiny closet, she fought the numbing urge to give up. Blood trickled down her face, forming puddles on the oak floorboards. She knew she didn't have the strength to overpower the intruder. Paralyzing fear and desperation were rendering her helpless to defend herself or attempt an escape.

Her mind raced as she sat huddled in the corner of the closet. Why was this happening to her? Why was God allowing this madman to threaten her life? At the same time she knew she needed God's help more than ever before. *Lord,* she prayed, *you promised to protect us from evil. Now I need your protection because I won't live unless you act.*

As she continued to pray, promises of God's comfort and presence filled her mind. Then the words of Psalm 18 came to her: "He delivered me from my strong enemy, and from those who hated me, for they were too mighty for me. . . . He brought me forth into a broad place; he rescued me, because he delighted in me." In that dark, small closet Eileen began to believe that somehow God would provide an escape.

As she slowly began to gain her strength she heard the faint bang of a door slamming shut. The house seemed completely silent. Had the attacker gone? Or was he waiting close by to pounce on her again? Feeling both desperation and renewed courage, she began to plot her way to safety. She knew she would have to act quickly.

Shoving against the closet door, she was able to push back the desk that had been propped against it to keep her inside. Emerging from the darkness of the closet, she edged toward the front window and saw the man struggling to load our television into his car. Heart pounding, she raced to the front door and locked it as securely as she could. Then she hurried to the phone in the entryway and anxiously waited for the operator's voice.

Hearing the cheery greeting of the phone operator, she began to weep, realizing that she had made contact with the outside world. Help would surely be on the way.

"Please help me, I've been beaten and robbed and I need the police," she sobbed into the phone.

"Where are you?" the person on the line asked urgently. Before Eileen could respond, a loud shout filled the hallway. She swung around to see the man's dark form against the glass section of the door.

"Where do you live?" asked the operator. Immobilized with fear, Eileen stood horrified as the front door splintered under the intruder's violent kicking and shoving.

As the door crashed open, she dropped the phone and fled out the back door, running for her life. Circling the house, she made it out to the street, where she approached a man walking down the sidewalk with a bag of groceries. He must have been shocked to see a young woman covered with blood, running toward him. "Help me, please help me!" she begged, but he stared straight ahead and kept right on walking.

We have all read the sad stories about uninvolved onlookers. But now it was Eileen who desperately needed help and there was none to be found. She felt as though time was running out. She felt certain that if she couldn't find help and refuge, the attacker would catch her and drag her back to our house where she might never escape again.

Frantically, Eileen hurried down the sidewalk to a small cluster of bungalows. One by one, she knocked on doors. She could sometimes hear footsteps and muted whispers inside. But no one answered. A tall concrete wall stood at the end of the walkway, barring any escape. She tried to hold back the panic at the thought of being trapped and totally alone to face this intruder.

With only two bungalows remaining, her hope momentarily soared as she heard a dead bolt slide open in response to her persistent knocking. A woman opened the door and cautiously peered out. "Yes?" she said, unable to resist recoiling in surprise at Eileen's bloody appearance.

"I've been beaten and robbed, please help me," she cried. The woman stood staring at her, momentarily unable to speak or move, then with sadness in her eyes she whispered, "I'm sorry, you can't come in—just go away." Eileen watched in disbelief as the door abruptly closed and the dead bolt slid back into place.

Where was God? Was he really powerful enough to rescue her from death? Or had he abandoned her to die, alone? Her mind was swirling with questions, doubts, and fears.

As she despairingly approached the last bungalow, she saw a man quickly advancing toward her with a gun in his hand. Before she even knew what was happening, he took her by the arm and led her into this last, lone home next to the high concrete wall. Had she escaped one killer only to be confronted by another? Exhausted and afraid, she slumped down in the chair he pointed to and leaned her head back against the cushion, bracing herself for whatever might come.

Looking up, her eyes focused on a uniform hanging from a hook on the wall. Then, in a quiet, reassuring voice, the man said, "You're all right now. I'm a police officer."

After a moment of disbelief, then relief, a feeble "Thank you" was all she could utter. As she sat there sobbing, safe at last, she began to realize that God had indeed rescued her in her greatest hour of need, and had provided a way of escape.

In a perfect world, that would have been the happy ending to a brief though harrowing experience. But we don't live in a perfect world, and the ramifications of our experiences can go on and on. The whole incident lasted only about forty minutes, but the scars still remain.

When I arrived on the scene, after receiving a phone call from one of the police officers, there were squad cars, an ambulance, even helicopters circling overhead. A policeman walked through the house with me, pointing out the blood-stains on the floor and walls. Standing by what remained of the shattered front door, he lowered his voice and firmly insisted that we board up the house, leave immediately, and move to a new place with no forwarding address, before the man returned "to finish the job." When I hesitated and told him that this seemed like a drastic reaction, he told me that if we insisted on staying, I would need to buy a gun. Should the attacker return, I was told to shoot him immediately. "If he falls forward into the house, call the police right away. But if he falls backward onto the porch, drag his body into the house and then call us." We moved, never spending another night in that house.

Following the attack there were years of struggles with fear, anxiety, and anger. The intruder was never caught, so there was never any closure or justice for Eileen. That lack of resolution kept her anxious and fearful that he might return at any moment.

Post-traumatic stress reactions, such as Eileen's inability to feel safe being home alone, have been woven into the fabric of our lives. There were many issues to work through and questions to explore. Why did God allow this to happen? How could people refuse to help? Would we ever feel safe again?

Of course healing comes and life goes on. But the scars, internal and external, don't just disappear.

Emotional Shock

There are experiences in life that are so significant in terms of inflicting pain their ramifications can last an entire lifetime. Just as our bodies experience shock when traumatized, so do our emotions. When someone is involved in a car accident, it is not uncommon for them to get out of the car, walk around, provide assistance, and talk lucidly with police or paramedics. They might even appear surprisingly calm and alert, with no visible indication of injury. In reality they may be suffering shock, which is the body's defense mechanism in the face of trauma. Adrenaline pumps through the body, providing short-term energy boosts and what seems like alertness and clarity of mind, when in actuality the body is shutting down in self-preservation. A similar result is evidenced when a person experiences emotional trauma.

Emotional trauma or shock involves a specific emotionally painful situation or event that causes a wound that affects our lives into the future. The effect of the trauma is demonstrated in behavior changes or reactions that live on long after the actual event.

Eileen's experience of post-traumatic stress disorder (PTSD) was demonstrated in fear responses that became part of her life. Entering a room of strangers, she would unconsciously survey the room to identify potential threats. Sometimes while dining in a restaurant, she would notice someone who might bear a slight resemblance to her attacker. Perhaps it was the person's height, posture, or merely a physical similarity. Suddenly, a wave of tension would engulf her body and fear would compel her to suddenly run out of the restaurant. I'd be left at the table to pay the check and try to get some of our meal in doggie bags to finish at home.

Emotional shock with the ensuing PTSD shows itself in several consistent ways. Years after the actual traumatic event, there can remain deep feelings of insecurity, confusion, irrational fear and distrust, unquenchable grief, and in many cases a profound sense of being disconnected from God. Because shock inhibits our thought processes and perception, there can also be difficulties with intimacy and self-esteem.

When these symptoms surface, they may no longer be connected in the person's mind to the actual trauma experience. Thus instead of working to resolve the traumatic experience, the person might assume, "I'm just nervous or jumpy," "The world is dangerous and I must stay vigilant," or "I don't feel God's love in my life and I'm spiritually dry."

If you are experiencing some or all of these symptoms, it might be helpful to look into your near or distant past to assess the possibility of emotional trauma. Working through the issues related to that event can release you from the ongoing stress and strain of trying to maintain self-preservation in a world of never-ending possible threats.

Trauma can come from a wide variety of situations, including loss of a loved one, a home, or a job; financial ruin or bankruptcy; diagnosis of disease or mental illness; an assault, rape, or violent attack; onset of terminal illness; and miscarriage during pregnancy or the death of a child or spouse. These and many more events can cause emotional shock, the effects of which impact us for years, causing reactions and responses that inhibit the growth and freedom we deserve.

Stages of Grief for Emotional Trauma

The stages of grief are well known and well documented ever since Elizabeth Kübler-Ross first published her book *On Death and Dying*.[1] While they are applicable in most of our grief experiences, they are particularly relevant to getting past emotional shock and trauma.

Stage 1: Denial

When we experience a traumatic event, it is not unusual for the shock to include denial. Denial is a natural protection that gives us a chance to process and come to terms with a painful, hurtful circumstance. We might give ourselves messages that this is not really happening to us, or that it is a nightmare from which we will wake and find everything to be all right. You may not want to even think about it, much less have friends ask how you are doing. Recognizing that it did happen, and it wasn't something you wanted or chose to have happen, allows you to realize that there are important choices and decisions to be made in order to get past the situation.

Stage 2: Anger

As the denial begins to fade away and the stark reality of the painful situation comes into focus, we can find ourselves transitioning from denial to anger. In a state of shock, we initially blame ourselves. Either we caused it or it was our fault, by our action or inaction. The seeds for regret are planted in this stage. We might ruminate on "If only I had . . ." or "If only I hadn't . . ." Of course we often blame ourselves. It is true that we most likely weren't perfect and made mistakes, even foolish ones, and everyone involved would do well to take responsibility for their own actions. However, establishing blame doesn't ease pain or end suffering.

When we least expect it, we can be swept up in the overwhelming floodwaters of emotional reactions expressed in anger and rage. As we review events and interactions leading up to the trauma, we can be stunned by the intensity of the emotions that swirl inside us. Particularly our anger and rage might surprise us, because until now we never thought of ourselves as an angry person.

We may be startled by our feelings of anger directed at those who wounded us, "by their betrayal and cruelty," as well as others who weren't directly involved, "but should have done something." We might feel resentment toward those whom we considered friends, assuming they knew what was happening yet didn't warn us. Sometimes we turn our anger on ourselves for not recognizing the signs of trouble and either stopping it or taking action to protect ourselves or our families. And it isn't uncommon for victims of emotional trauma to rage at God, wondering, "Why did you let this happen to me?"

Underneath the feelings of anger and rage is a depth of pain and sorrow that must be recognized and allowed to come out in order to get past the pain.

Underneath the feelings of anger and rage is a depth of pain and sorrow that must be recognized and allowed to come out in order to get past the pain. Because of this hurt we may feel a wide range of strong and sometimes frightening feelings. Unfortunately when we are in shock it is not unusual to lose sight of what is being felt. We can become so out of touch that all we know is we feel "bad," "mad," or "sad." It might be helpful to write a list of as many feelings as possible that you might be experiencing during this time of recovery. You might be surprised by the number and variety of possible feelings swirling around in you at any given time.

You might feel some of these: annoyance, frustration, criticalness, impatience, jealousy, disgust, rage, love, relief, sadness, fear, resentment, confusion, as well as self-pity, loneliness, shame, guilt, numbness, hopelessness, irritation, and just plain regret. When we allow ourselves to experience each of the many feelings connected to the traumatic event, we are better able to release our emotional energy instead of keeping it bottled up inside. As the power of turbulent emotional energy gets diffused in healthy ways, we in turn begin to feel more relaxed and less churned up, and are able to think with more clarity about the next steps forward in our life.

Stage 3: Bargaining

The next phase in the stages of grief is bargaining. Initially this might be the first step toward striking deals that might temporarily help a person cope. Being in a state of emotional shock, the injured person might be inclined to agree to anything in hopes of ending the pain or resuming the relationship. Agreements negotiated in this phase are usually short-term and provide only temporary space from which long-term agreements can be made. Of course bargaining with God is not uncommon, as we seek anything to help end the trauma and stop the pain.

In time we often see that bargains struck while in a state of emotional shock are not what are finally agreed upon. Thus in the case of a divorce, initially a spouse might give up anything and sometimes everything, hoping to save the marriage; when it becomes apparent that it won't be saved, they change into possessive and demanding negotiators. Still, bargaining can be an initial first step in a decision-making process that helps the person cope temporarily with their trauma.

Stage 4: Depression

Depression can be a debilitating condition that affects every part of the trauma victim's life. The reality and extent of loss, coupled with the realization that what was lost will not return, can cause a person to sink deeply into the mire of hopelessness and pain. When we find ourselves in this depression stage, we may be surprised how difficult it might become to handle simple tasks, function on a day-to-day basis, or even just get up in the morning. Fortunately there is professional help available to enable us to cope and get through this part of recovery without self-destruction or suicide. In some ways we can find hope, knowing that this depression may indicate we are almost through the stages of grief. There is only one more stage to experience.

Stage 5: Acceptance

When we go through a traumatic incident, we might think that it couldn't get any worse. It isn't uncommon, however, for traumatized feelings actually to increase over time. This may happen partially because of our inability to accept the circumstance and let go of the painful experience. Acceptance frees us from the cycle of reliving the experience. With acceptance comes strength to move forward in life, as we begin to accept what happened and make the choice to live in spite of the loss and pain.

Acceptance doesn't necessarily mean we have forgotten about it. C. S. Lewis observed, "Part of every misery is, so to speak, the misery's shadow or reflection: the fact that you don't merely suffer but have to keep on thinking about the fact that you suffer. I not only live each endless day in grief, but live each day thinking about living each day in grief."[2]

Even if it were possible to forget, it probably wouldn't be healthy to neatly tuck our pain away somewhere in our mental closets. Neither does it mean that everything is okay now. It does, however, mean that you are okay, and are choosing to get past what you'll never get over.

It takes time to experience these stages and come through the other side. Give yourself time to heal, and in time you will find your life free from the debilitating hold of emotional trauma and shock. Some people experience these grief stages in a progression, but others find their experience isn't linear at all; rather, they feel as if they bounced from stage to stage, even returning to a previous stage as if they were visiting an old friend.

I believe breakthroughs come when we finally let go of wanting to change the past.

I believe breakthroughs come when we finally let go of wanting to change the past. A sense of closure comes when we finally allow ourselves to accept the reality that what was done is done, and nothing will bring back the past or undo the damage. Jesus's final words as he died on the cross were, "It is finished." While our pain can in no way be compared to his, the realization that in fact *it is finished* can be our harbinger of a whole new beginning.

6

Fear

The Tie That Binds

I learned that courage was not the absence of fear,
but the triumph over it.

Nelson Mandela

Fear may be the one thing every person in the world has in common. For some it is a sharp and debilitating pain, while others conceal their fear under a façade of bravado. Regardless of our exterior appearance, we all experience fear and we need to discover fresh ways to live in spite of it.

Fear affects us in myriad ways. It can hinder our personal and professional growth, block intimacy and inhibit relationships, and cause us to withdraw and disengage from the adventure of life. Fear of God may keep us from experiencing spiritual wholeness, and fear of the world may keep us from experiencing life to its fullest.

Our fears can surface from time to time in vague and anxious thoughts or they can be very specific, overwhelming us with full-blown panic attacks causing us to flee, disengage, or even collapse. Fear is a response to a perceived threat, real or imagined. If it is real, then we might consider an entirely rational fear as one in which there is good reason to be afraid. It is a healthy, positive fear because it serves to warn us of impending danger so we can take steps to meet or avoid the challenge in appropriate ways. In the face of a real threat, fear is a gift, one that can mobilize us to action and protect us from harm.

Anxiety is often confused with fear. It feels similar, but it is the result of our reaction to an undefined, unknown threat or danger. Dealing with anxiety or panic attacks, our body can undergo the same physical reactions experienced when we are afraid of a known threat, and they are many and varied: increased heart rate, difficulty breathing, sharp abdominal pain, headaches, increased blood pressure, twitching, or dry mouth. Other symptoms might include numbness, back ache, a quivering voice, fatigue, or shakiness. Fear affects us physically as well as mentally, emotionally, and spiritually.

And then there are fears that grip people for no particular reason, and these are called phobias. They are considered irrational fears. The most common phobia is said to be public speaking, but there are limitless possible phobias including some that are quite common and some that are rare and unusual. They range from claustrophobia, a fear of tight places, to social anxiety disorder, which is a fear of interacting with other people, to a fear of heights, fear of spiders, and even a fear of packing. Some people fear physical threats, but there is also fear of the unknown, or fear of loss, abandonment, inadequacy, or humiliation. Try googling "phobia" and marvel at the sheer number and variety of very real and debilitating fears we can experience on a daily basis.

For the person experiencing a phobic reaction, it doesn't matter whether it is rational or irrational, real or unreal. The impact is great.

There are also various kinds of fear. It is futile to attempt to persuade another person that they shouldn't be afraid. Fear is a feeling. It isn't a criminal act or a character flaw. Any attempt to talk someone out of their fear is meaningless and a huge waste of time. Feelings are not logical, they are merely experienced. Our attempt at persuasion might make sense to us and even to the other person, but it rarely brings about change. Feelings cannot be reasoned with or argued away.

Our upbringing and experiences can determine our fear responses. Growing up as a child in Cameroon, West Africa, I developed a fear of insects. Little, harmless bugs creep me out. My wife and son are always stepping in to take care of a little spider or crawly thing while I cower as far away as possible until the horrible monster is removed from the house.

When Damian was young, I took him to see the movie *Arachnophobia*, starring John Goodman as the exterminator. I felt confident that I could watch this harmless film without any undue stress. I didn't realize that with every passing moment I grew more nervous and tense.

At one point in the movie Damian quietly reached over and tickled the back of my hand. I leapt out of my seat, screaming in shock and terror. Of course, when I jumped I accidently knocked off my eyeglasses, sending them flying across the dark theater. The theatergoers were laughing as I crawled around on my hands and knees looking for my lost glasses.

My fear of insects is completely irrational, of course, but it is quite real to me and is probably based on past experiences. My insect and spider phobias, I think, are probably due to my early years of waking up in Africa and seeing the mosquito nets over my bed completely covered with all manner of creatures not found in *National Geographic*. Varieties of frightening insects, including praying mantis-like creatures nearly a foot long, loomed right over my face while I tried to determine if it was worth getting up to face another day.

Phobias are irrational. For example, I may be afraid of insects, but the odd thing is I love snakes. Unlike Indiana Jones, a character with a morbid fear of snakes, they don't bother me at all. As kids we had snakes for pets. My brother Richard used to order them from exotic snake farms in Florida, to be shipped to our house in California. When I hear that someone is afraid of snakes, I laugh in disbelief. Who could be afraid of those cuddly creatures?

Fear or Excitement?

Physical and emotional responses to fear are so varied and inexplicable they can be similar to the reactions a person feels when they are on an adventure or are very excited about something. When we are excited and don't perceive a threat or danger, we can go through the symptoms of a fear reaction without its negative or debilitating aspects. A teenager who isn't afraid of thrill rides gets joyful exhilaration from the experience at an amusement park while their hesitant parent can be paralyzed with fear while sitting next to them on the same ride. What makes the difference? It is their perception of danger or awareness of possible threat. If we prepare ourselves to embrace the adventure of living, we may end up experiencing more excitement and less fear.

Remember the old saying "ignorance is bliss"? There is an element of truth to this bit of wisdom when it comes to getting past our fears. If we lack experience or insight about some perilous situation that arises, we often can go through it with a surprising amount of tranquility. People around us who are more knowledgeable about the circumstances and the impending danger may be stressing out, but we can experience the adventure without fear.

One summer I was invited to join my longtime friends Randy and Bruce on a boat trip. We were going to leave from Seattle, sail through the San Juan Islands, cruise up through the Northwest Passage, and float right to Alaska. I was excited to be part of this three-man adventure because I had never been on a boat before and I was ready for something new and exciting in my life. I'll never forget the beauty of nature and the camaraderie of friends sharing a once-in-a-lifetime experience. That is, until we started to sink in the cold Alaskan waters.

Because I had never been a sailor, everything was new to me. I marveled at the skill and knowledgeable confidence demonstrated by Captain Randy and Navigator Bruce. My important tasks consisted of climbing around the deck in the rain to secure the lines. I also had the privilege of cooking all the meals in the galley and cleaning the cabin and the head (bathroom). Together we were a great team.

When the time came to leave the shelter of the Inland Passage and cross the open sea of the Straits of Queen Charlotte, we got up early to check weather conditions and height of the sea waves, and to pray for safety on this, the riskiest part of the trip. Randy knew that it would take all day, and it would most likely be a turbulent experience on the open sea, but I was excited to get going. We bobbed along, pushing through the waves for hours without seeing another boat anywhere. It was intriguing for me to think of us all alone on the open sea, like the nursery rhyme, "Rub a dub dub, three men in a tub."

We were making good progress, on the lookout for submerged logs that might collide with the boat. When I climbed down to the main cabin for a snack, I noticed water slowly filling the room. I called out to Randy, asking if this was a normal phenomenon on a boat, since I had no experience. He flew down the steps, took a quick look at the rising water, and raced to the ship's radio to call the Coast Guard. Something you really don't want to hear on a boat in the middle of nowhere is "Mayday."

He was able to tell our location to the Coast Guard, but they informed us they were several hours away, and that they would not get to our location in time for a rescue. The dispatcher overheard me ask Randy what I should do in the meantime. He suggested Randy have me get a bucket and bail water out of the small window in the head. "It won't help," he told him, "but it will keep your friend busy and out of the way." Accordingly, Randy gave me the task—but not the reason behind it. While I went searching for a bucket, the Coast Guard broadcast an all points bulletin for any vessel in the vicinity to come to our aid. About then the boat ran out of gas.

Evidently the boat had two gas tanks, but the switch that changed tanks wasn't working, so we were unable to switch to the second tank. That was about the time we discovered that the bilge pumps weren't working either. Bruce patiently explained to me that we could stay afloat if the pumps kept emptying the water as it entered the hull of the boat. But without their help we just took on more and more water.

This was all quite exciting, but I wasn't worried, since I had a lifejacket to keep me afloat should the boat sink. Of course I hadn't yet learned that in the frigid Alaskan waters a person would have only about eight minutes until hypothermia set in. I was told later that the lifejackets are there so that they could find our bodies.

Although we hadn't seen any other boats all day, and our boat was bobbing helplessly while taking on water, suddenly several different vessels approached us. First a huge fishing trawler on its way from Alaska to Seattle came up and informed us they had a pump on board that could be used to pump out the water in our boat. Their only concern was that because of the size of their ship, they might capsize us if they attempted to come alongside with the pump.

A smaller fishing boat approached and they offered to get the pump from the large boat and bring it to us, which seemed like a good idea. Then out of nowhere a young couple on a trip around the world in their sailboat came alongside. They put the bow of their sailboat into the side of our boat to keep us from drifting.

The husband climbed onto our boat, pulled up the floorboards in the cabin, and jumped down into the water-filled hull of our boat. He soon surfaced and began grabbing an assortment of stuff, such as shirts, pencils, and plastic bags, which he made into a makeshift plug. He dove back down into the cold water and shoved this temporary plug into the hole in the bottom of our boat, effectively shutting off the geyser that was spouting water through the hull. Shivering from the cold, he climbed back into the cabin.

Eventually, the pump did its work, the "plug" held, and cans of gasoline were poured into our empty tank so we could resume our trek northward to rendezvous with the Coast Guard vessel. I was surprised when the boats involved in helping us all turned and followed us on our way. A couple of fishermen stayed on board our boat, so I asked them why they didn't head back the way they were going, now that we were apparently saved.

"It's the rule of the sea," they told me. "When a ship is in trouble we stay with it until released by the Coast Guard. After all, today it was you, but tomorrow it might be one of our boats that needs assistance." One by one, the Coast Guard released the boats as we got closer to their rescue vessel.

At last we connected with the Coast Guard and were led to a remote island, which had a repair facility with a few rooms to rent and a small café. By now it was late at night and we were tired, hungry, and relieved to be on dry ground. The waitress came out of the café and told us that they were usually closed by this time of night, but they had been following our progress on their radio. Entering the warm dining room, I heard Bruce tell the waitress, "We almost died today."

When I heard those words, I was shocked. It had never crossed my mind that we were in any real danger. To me, it just seemed like an adventurous experience that surely was a normal part of boating. Randy had done an exceptional job of taking charge and making sure we were given the best opportunity for rescue. No one seemed to panic. In fact, just the opposite: everyone acted like this was business as usual, merely taking care to remedy any difficulties as they surfaced. Because of this I was happily oblivious to the real danger we faced.

Of course, when I heard that we had almost died that day, everything changed inside me. Immediately I was gripped with fear and anxiety. I tossed and turned through the night, wondering about the impending danger and already fearing the time when the boat would be fixed and we would have to continue our voyage. Now that I was safe, and more aware, I was paralyzed with fear. I wished I didn't know now what I didn't know then.

Reflecting on this experience, I began to see that fear is not very different from excitement or adventure. The difference is in our attitude toward the experience. Because I didn't know enough to be afraid, I assumed that our potential disaster was merely an accepted aspect of boating. Because my friends didn't show panic or hysteria, I went through the whole day marveling at their problem-solving abilities and creative efforts to keep us afloat.

How different it might have been if Randy or Bruce began to scream or weep or behave in panic-stricken ways. I might have jumped overboard and tried to swim to shore just to get away from the sinking ship. But they had appeared to take everything in stride, so I was calm and intrigued by the efforts going on all around me.

Repeatedly in the Bible, people are told to not fear. When angels announced the birth of Jesus to the shepherds on the hillside, their first words were "Fear not." Repeatedly Jesus chided his closest friends about their fear. He often asked, "Why are you afraid?" It is almost as if God knows that we will often feel fear whether or not there is any real danger.

We can live adventurous lives, embracing the excitement of growth and change without becoming trapped in the debilitating grip of fear. On the sinking ship, I wasn't fully aware of the danger because I had the mindset (naively) that what we were experiencing was unusual for me as a landlubber, but was probably a normal occurrence for experienced sailors.

If Bruce had shouted, "We're going to die!" when he saw the water rising in the cabin, I might have responded quite differently. There would have been good reason for my fear response. But because he didn't panic, I didn't either. There are many times when we get our fear clues from people around us. In a culture of suspicion, distrust, and fear, we will tune in to clues about how we should respond. Likewise, in a climate of reasonable problem solving even high-risk situations can energize us and empower us to face new challenges.

We can live adventurous lives, embracing the excitement of growth and change without becoming trapped in the debilitating grip of fear.

Fear can be as contagious as a viral infection. Groups of people can be seduced to panic by the acts or words of a few fearful people. However, the reverse is also true. People have acted with great courage and inner strength in the face of seemingly overwhelming opposition. The difference lies in the choice we make to accept hardship as a challenge to embrace rather than a threat from which we should recoil.

Each of us has a different tolerance for excitement. We also have our own perceptions about what we should fear. A more helpful strategy is to acknowledge another person's feelings of fear, and encourage that person by pointing out how courageous they are to face these fears. Then look for ways to test reality, helping the person determine if indeed there is a threat, or if it is an opportunity for you both to experience a new adventure.

Occupations and Preoccupations

When something happens in our lives we feel stressed; we get burdened, we get busy, we get occupied. Your occupation is what fills your time. For some of us it's a job. Others find a creative passion or interest into which to pour themselves.

We can also be occupied without having a job per se. In a men's group we were discussing our various occupations when someone mentioned that one of the group members was retired and therefore didn't have an occupation. The older man became indignant, pointing out that although he wasn't working full time, there were more demands on his time and energy now than there were when he was in corporate life. "There is no such thing as retirement," he insisted, "because we all have to work full time to make life meaningful." I realized that, retired or not, he's busy with his occupation.

Most of us find it easy to talk with people about our occupations, but what about our preoccupations? The word *preoccupation* sounds like it is the work we do before we go to work. In a sense, that is true. A preoccupation is how you fill your time with what will be happening in the future by worrying about it now. We can be occupied with today and yet preoccupied with tomorrow. No wonder we have stress. There's not enough time or creative energy for us to deal with both today and tomorrow.

Our preoccupations fill our minds, fill our hearts, and irritate our stomachs because we can't deal with them yet— they are in the future. Preoccupation turns into worry, which results in anxiety. Preoccupation creates its own stress because we worry that we won't be ready, prepared, or adequate to face the future. After all we're barely making it through today. Our preoccupations constantly remind us of whom we forgot to write or call or visit, and it's all waiting for us and looming larger and larger. We can feel overwhelmed and exhausted just thinking about what we may have to face. When we're overwhelmed with worry, it can seem ludicrous that in Philippians 4:6 Paul has the audacity to say, "Do not be anxious about anything." Henri Nouwen wrote:

> One of the most notable characteristics of worrying is it fragments our lives. The many things to do, to think about, to plan for, the many people to remember to visit, to talk with, the many causes to attack or defend, all these pull us apart and make us lose our center. Worrying causes us to be all over the place but seldom at home.[1]

Getting Past Our Fear

A natural response when we experience fear is to withdraw. When we perceive possible hurt or threat we tend to pull away for self-protection. The same is true when we have phobias, anxiety, or worry. Unfortunately, while that may lower the intensity of our feelings for a time, it doesn't help us get past our fear in a lasting way. Gestalt therapists encourage their patients to move toward their fears. When fear is confronted and observed, it can be overcome and set aside.

Of course this idea didn't begin with Gestalt therapists. "Do the thing you fear most," Mark Twain advised, "and the death of fear will follow."[2] I think that for the most part

Mark Twain was mistaken. I realize that many people who are terrified of public speaking, which reportedly is number one on phobia lists, have found great help in overcoming their fear from organizations like Toastmasters, which encourage and practice doing the thing you fear most. However, I don't believe the fear dies. Rather, we face the fear and live in spite of it. Even after a successful experience of facing our fear, it will be waiting for us the next time we step out of our comfort zone.

I have many fears that are irrational, and quite a few that seem logical to me. My morbid fear of heights doesn't make sense to anyone, but rationally knowing that hasn't helped me climb any higher. I get sweaty palms just looking at a photo of the Grand Canyon, much less walking out over the abyss in the glass-bottomed viewing chamber. Despite my ever-present fear, I have tried to live beyond its grip. Pressure to be a good dad led me to suffer through the horrific climb up the circular ladder to the top of the Statue of Liberty, before it was closed to tourists.

I still remember the night Damian asked me to take him up to the top of the Eiffel Tower in Paris. I clung tightly to the rickety bars of the ancient elevator as we lurched and clanged our way inch by inch into the French night. Arriving at the lookout level, I held back, crouching against a wall while Damian ran around begging me to join him on the edge of oblivion.

Of course the cog train to the top of the glacier above Zermatt nearly induced cardiac arrest, which would have left Damian fatherless, and it would have been his own fault. At the very top of the mountain we walked out on the icy peak, looking down at the Alps below, and I began to hyperventilate and lose consciousness. I'm even feeling dizzy as I write about this. Damian was laughing and running on the glacier, while I tried to maintain consciousness long enough to keep him from sliding off the mountain to a certain doom. But as I tried to corral the boy, I had to keep stopping to breathe into our lunch sack to keep from passing out.

I still regret agreeing to have a board retreat at a center that specialized in team-building exercises at a Santa Cruz conference center. As the leader, I went along to encourage the others and participate in the dialogue, but I had no intention of doing anything crazy like flying through the forest on zip lines.

I survived most of the weekend without being personally involved, until the peer pressure got too great and I was compelled to do one "trust" exercise. All I had to do was climb up a giant tree to a height of about three stories and leap off a tiny platform to grab hold of a trapeze that would safely lower me to the ground. Besides, I was wearing a safety harness, so I knew nothing would go wrong.

It didn't matter how many others had climbed and jumped before me. It didn't matter that I carefully buckled the harness around my body. It didn't matter that my fear was completely irrational and I had a wonderful teaching opportunity to demonstrate leadership with the others on our team. Nothing mattered to me but the fear.

It took a long time for me to get up the tree trunk, and that wasn't even the scary part. Climbing out on the tiny platform was accomplished only with the tenacity of an inchworm. But jumping out to a little trapeze? That was insane. Whose idea was this retreat? A crowd gathered below, shouting encouragement that reminded me of scenes in movies where the jumper is on the ledge of a skyscraper and the crowd below is shouting for him not to jump. Then I did it. Leaping out into space, I grabbed the trapeze—which happened to be wet and slippery—and lost hold to fall help-lessly to earth. I was saved only by the alert guide who used my harness ropes to break my fall before I went splat.

I expected that after facing my fear and showing extraordinary courage in spite of it, I would have defeated my phobia and could now live free from my irrational fear of heights. But that didn't happen. The next time I rode the huge glass elevator at the Mall of the Americas, I clung to the wall with the buttons, which was as far away from the glass as I could get. I'm still fearful because the fear is irrational. It doesn't go away.

> *If we wait until our fear is gone before we step out, we will never take the first step.*

If that is so, what is the benefit of facing our fear and going toward it, and doing the thing we fear most? The benefit is that while we won't get over it we will, in these experiences, get past it. We will experience a fuller life in spite of our fear. I shared adventures with my son that we will never forget, and it was done in spite of my fear. If we wait until our fear is gone before we step out, we will never take the first step.

Maybe we should be grateful for fear. It's been a warning system that alerts us to impending danger throughout our lives. Without fear we would have no early warning defense system against evil. Fear is a common bond holding all of humanity in its shared grasp. Without fear we would never know what it is to be courageous.

Perhaps fear is the GPS that shows us the path that can lead us past what we'll never get over.

7

Regret

The Heart's Bungee Cord

If only. Those must be the two saddest words in
the world.

Mercedes Lackey

I was never into bungee jumping. My great fear of heights,
combined with a passion to keep living, has kept me from
hurtling my body headfirst off a precipice or bridge in what
some consider to be the ultimate adrenaline rush. I have many
friends who love to bungee jump and they are enthusiastic,
describing their experiences in such graphic detail that I get
sweaty palms just listening.

One of the first things they mention is how terrified they
are before jumping. That is followed by an exhilarating few
seconds of total freefall as they plummet headfirst down,

down, down toward the hard ground or sometimes the river below. Finally the cord reaches its full extension and snaps back like a giant rubber band, yanking them right back up the way they came. This lift, they tell me, feels like flying as they soar skyward until their body weight combines with gravity right at the top of the rise and once more they plunge headlong toward the earth.

Who needs bungee jumping? Not me. I can experience the same frightening emotions because I have regrets that yank me back from whatever adventure I'm pursuing and send me soaring back to the old hurts, losses, and miseries. Regrets are the bungee cords of our hearts.

The feeling of regret can almost haunt us in unsuspecting moments. Our mind drifts and finally settles on "what ifs" and "if onlys" that have the power to pull us back into a past that never really existed.

When we are caught up in regret, it is easy to lose touch with reality because our memories and the feelings associated with our memories are so strong. It is important to remember that what we think or feel about the past and what it actually was are two distinct and different things. Lost in the irresistible pull of regret, I can recall an event, a conversation, or a relationship and it can replay in my mind over and over again. It all seems so clear in hindsight. However, what I am remembering may have little if anything to do with what actually did or didn't happen.

Our feelings of regret can flow from many differing experiences. It might relate to something we did, but it could equally apply to something we didn't do that in hindsight we wish we did. Words spoken or left unspoken can haunt us like a bad ghost story. Our lives are filled with decisions and choices.

We rarely know their full significance at the time. But years later, we might beat on ourselves for the choice we made.

Sometimes we have vague feelings of remorse about the past, but those are slightly different from regret, because feelings of regret are linked to very specific events in our past. Perhaps we wonder what would have happened if we had made a different choice. Everyone has grounds to reflect on choices made that turned out to have tremendous implications for today. We wonder, "How would my life be different if I had not turned down that job offer?" or "What if I had turned down that job offer or if I had said yes to that marriage proposal?" or "What if I had said no to that marriage proposal?"

Buyer's Remorse

Most of us know and understand the term *buyer's remorse.* This is the mysterious feeling that comes over people after they have made a big purchase decision. For example, we need to buy a car, so we look at various possibilities in our price range. Then we read articles in magazines and make note of the advantages of each car we are considering. Finally we narrow our choices down to two finalists. We banter with friends and family about the benefits and drawbacks of each until we finally reach a decision. Confident, we march into the dealership and buy the car that we have determined is the best choice. We drive it home, park it proudly in the driveway, and go to sleep relieved to have finally made the decision.

But the next morning, driving to work, we are suddenly overwhelmed with the sense that we made a huge mistake. *I shouldn't have bought this one! What was I thinking? Maybe it is not too late to take this car back and get the other one.* Salesmen understand buyer's remorse. They live with it continually. But they also know that it doesn't matter which car you decided to purchase—you will long for the other one. Buy the Ford, regret not getting the Chevy. Buy the Chevy, regret not getting the Ford. Buy both the Ford and the Chevy, regret not buying the Toyota. It doesn't matter which we choose, because the buyer's remorse will get us either way.

"I see it all perfectly," wrote existential philosopher Søren Kierkegaard. "There are two possible situations—one can either do this or that. My honest opinion and my friendly advice is this: do it or do not do it—you will regret both."[1]

The good news is that in time, we get over these feelings of remorse and we drive on with the car we purchased and block out of our memory any doubts we may have experienced during the buying process. Eventually all we remember is that we bought a car, no big deal. Many people who have occasional feelings of remorse find a way to deflect any lingering bad feelings so that they are able to live in the now. They do not experience the pull of regret yanking them back to an imagined past.

When Paul Anka wrote the song "My Way," he probably never realized it would become such an anthem to self-sufficiency. Frank Sinatra made it a classic as he sang about regrets. He evidently had a few of them, but not enough to bother mentioning. I sort of envy the singer's apparent ability to shrug off mistakes from the past. Life might be a little simpler if we just got over it. It certainly would be easier to glide through life never wondering about our past, the mistakes we made, or the hurt we caused. I guess it is possible for us to become so relationally callused that we are unaffected by the pain we receive and inflict on others. But that experience doesn't ring true for those of us who find ourselves suddenly yanked back in our minds to rehash old hurts and old decisions that fester in our minds, unresolved.

I haven't found any one word or expression to accurately describe the regret experience. Sadness, yearning, self-hate, self-pity, longing, and shame all come to mind. Perhaps a bit of all these feelings swirl around when we are pulled back into a painful past. Each of us experiences regret in our own unique way, yet there seems to be a common thread in the experience of regret.

Regret can begin quite simply with a casual thought or reminiscence about a specific event in our lives where we made a choice. Perhaps it was a decision to do something or not do something. We might have been faced with an opportunity, and now we think, *If I had only said yes instead of no.* . . . It is important to realize that these casual, seemingly unimportant things flash through our minds at unsuspecting times. We can be driving down the road when a certain song comes on the radio—and we are quite suddenly thinking of a previous experience.

The second phase in the experience of regret can appear quite positive. We momentarily think about the specific incident and tell ourselves we are going to get on with life and not think about this anymore. Good for us! We realize that no good can come from rehashing an old memory. This gives us a brief sense of well-being for having made a good response to the flash of memory.

Then the third phase comes along. Just as we relax and start to move forward in our mind, we are struck with an onslaught of poignant and painful memories accompanied by intense inner pain, as if we are being punished for our situation. This emotional tsunami can overwhelm us and propel us back to relive a painful part of our past.

When I was talking about this with a friend over lunch one day, he related how in his experience, the sudden flood of emotions and painful memories left him with the feeling of "being in shackles, like I'm chained in a dungeon and there's nothing I can do about it."

I believe this sense of oppressive pain related to our past is one of the most tragic aspects of regret. When we find ourselves dragged into this dark place in our minds, it leads us to a final stage of regret. This is a place of despair. Our minds are filled with distorted thinking and beliefs about ourselves and our lives. My friend described this stage as being almost in a trancelike state of unreality. "Picture yourself inside one of those old lava lamps from the hippie days. It is like you are floating—surrounded by all these blobs of emotion and thoughts and memories that keep rising up all around you. You think you are really seeing things clearly and that you deserve the pain, because your life is ruined and will never be good again."

Look for the Lies

This crippling punishment, which we inflict on ourselves too easily, can become a substitute for healthy living. In time, the regret for the things we did will diminish. However, it is more difficult to get past the regret for the things we didn't do.

Not all regret is connected to pain. Sometimes regret involves a missed opportunity that will never come again, or a decision that might have impacted life in significant ways.

One of the strongest pulls of regret is for missed joy, or blessings refused along the way.

When I finished graduate studies, we relocated to a small beach community north of San Diego. We moved into a duplex, which we shared with an elderly couple. The man was a golf nut. I'd hear him watching golf on TV, and talking about golf continually over the phone and with visitors. He even made clubs in his garage, which had been turned into a workshop.

As long as we lived next door, he tried to talk me into letting him teach me how to play golf, but I told him it was a dumb game and I was not interested. He insisted that he could help me learn to play excellently, and he would even make me a custom set of clubs if only I'd let him teach me the game. I made it clear that I wasn't going to learn to play golf and I didn't want his help. Eventually they moved to Mexico City, where he had been hired to teach the president of Mexico.

Years later, I became fascinated with golf, but I was a terrible player. A golf pro told me that I was a mess of compensations, each one trying to compensate for some other thing that I did wrong (not unlike my life). Once in frustration I even prayed about it. I asked God why he didn't give me the ability to play on a higher level. The next day I was reading an issue of *Golf Digest* that featured an interview with Jack Nicklaus. In the interview, Jack shared his appreciation for his lifetime teacher and friend, Jack Grout, who had coached him from his teenage years all through his professional career.

Suddenly I felt sick to my stomach. I called out, "Eileen, we were living next door to Jack Grout and he wanted to teach me to play golf, and I told him to leave me alone because I didn't want his help!"

My mind raced. How could I have been so stupid? What if I had let him teach me? Maybe I'd be a professional golfer today. How could I have missed a golden opportunity of a lifetime that had simply been offered to me, no strings attached? I regret my mistake every time I set foot on a golf course. Every time I swing a club and listen to the snickers and heckling of my buddies, I feel regret. Of course I realize that this may be a small and insignificant thing to regret, but it is still real. Knowing that my unique combination of ignorance and arrogance joined together to cause me to turn away from what I now know to be a chance of a lifetime still stings.

> *That sense of missing out because we passed up our only chance of happiness holds us captive—because we believe the lies.*

That sense of missing out because we passed up our only chance of happiness holds us captive—because we believe the lies. Although we may be oblivious, other people can help us see the lies and deceptions in our mind. In the grip of regret our understanding becomes clouded and we assume the worst about ourselves. We start to believe that we are unlovable, that we are no good, that we are not the leader or even the person we thought we were. These lies can be recognized and put aside so that the truth about ourselves can take hold of us.

In the Lord of the Rings film based on J. R. R. Tolkien's novel *The Two Towers*, Gandalf the White makes his way into the throne room of King Théoden of Rohan. But instead of finding a strong leader, he sees a pathetic old man seated on the throne, staring through lifeless eyes while the evil adviser Grima Wormtongue continually whispers lies into his ear. In this insightful scene, Gandalf rises up and casts out the lies from the mind of the king, and we watch as the pitiful ruler begins to transform from his weak, delusional state of mind until he is once more strong, powerful, and free from the lies that poisoned his thoughts and weakened his spirit.[2]

The grip of regret grows as it feeds on lies and delusion. There can be no freedom in life while we are imprisoned in the shackles of regret. Jesus said, "You will know the truth and the truth will set you free" (John 8:32). If you are not experiencing freedom, and are bound by regret, it may be time to allow the truth of God's love and power to permeate your mind. In the same way that the king needed Gandalf to come and release him from the prison of his own mind, we need people in our lives who will lovingly and courageously interrupt our cycle of regret and release us from the lies.

We are made to be in relationship with one another and with God. Regret tends to pull us out of healthy relationships and into greater and greater isolation. This isolation increases our sense of loneliness, which only serves to intensify our regret. Thus we need people in our life who are committed to speaking the truth in love so that we can begin to rediscover reality in our heart and mind.

I'm very fortunate to have Joe as a friend. I first met Joe years ago when he was a young man with a keen business mind and an energetic spirit. I moved out of state and didn't see him for many years, though I heard about his life from mutual friends. We were excited to hear about his founding of an outdoor clothing company that rode a wave of popularity and financial success in its years of rapid growth. His work allowed him to travel extensively through many exotic lands. Then, at a fairly early age, Joe sold his interests in the company and retired with enough money to live well the rest of his life. He and I eventually reconnected, and began to meet for breakfast on a regular basis.

One of the things we noticed as we began to share about our lives was that, years before, he had perceived me as a successful author and speaker with an exciting life and rapidly growing ministry while he was struggling with issues of faith, finances, career, and women. Now it seemed as if our roles were reversed. He was on top of the world, and I was living with deep regrets about what I perceived as a collapse of confidence and the negative effect it had on my life. I felt like my family and I were struggling to start over with very little of anything.

I felt emotionally adrift, held captive in the dungeon of regret, rerunning the mental tapes of my own perceived failure and rehashing experiences that I considered as betrayal. I'm sure it was boring to be around me because I kept talking through the lens of my pain and loss instead of considering the positive options all around me.

Joe's insight shocked me. "Have you ever considered that it was important for you to go through some of the painful things you have experienced? Maybe it wasn't a mistake, but perhaps it was an important experience to get you where God wanted you to be all along," he said. I wondered what he was talking about. How could it have been necessary or needed or good in any sense of the word? That seemed completely crazy from my perspective.

"Just look at it from a different perspective," he said, with a gleam in his eye. "What if God had always wanted you to come back to Seattle and start a new church with a creative approach to ministry in a relational, authentic way?

Is there any way you would have considered leaving your old life to come here and start over from scratch? No way. You never would have even considered the idea, much less prayed about it or explored the possibility with those close to you." I knew he was right about that. I'd never have given up my secure and established life to do something risky like church planting.

It just takes looking at the situation from a slightly different angle for reality to start to shine through.

"Maybe you had to go through the painful experiences in order to come here and start the new church—which may be one of the most meaningful chapters of your entire life! Have you thought of that, John?" Joe sat back while I muttered, "No, I never thought of that."

It took a while before I could see the wisdom in my friend's words. I was held captive by regret, and I needed someone to interrupt me with a new perspective. Looking back, I wonder if I was a little bit like Jonah, not willing to go and do what the Lord desired for him. If God could use a terrible storm, a boatload of sailors, and a giant fish to get Jonah's attention, surely he could use a good dose of pain and heartache to get me where I needed to be.

It just takes looking at the situation from a slightly different angle for reality to start to shine through. Alexander Graham Bell is quoted as saying, "When one door closes, another opens; but we often look so long and so regretfully upon the closed door that we do not see the one which has opened for us."[3]

While we may not get over what we regret, we can get past it. Perhaps it is as simple as turning away long enough to discover the next opportunity waiting for us. It probably won't be the same opportunity, and it will feel different, but it can be good and fulfilling when we step toward it.

I looked through the Bible to find what God has to say about bungee cords. Yes, I know, bungee cords are not discussed all that much in the Bible, but if regret is the heart's bungee cord, pulling us back into distorted reality and overwhelming pain, what is God's alternative? How will the Lord counter the relentless pull of our emotional bungee cord?

Then I read a passage that caught my attention. In Hosea 11 the Lord says, "I led them with cords of human kindness, with ties of love" (v. 4). Then it hit me. The antidote for the pull of regret is experiencing the even stronger counterforce of being pulled by divine cords of human kindness and love.

When we are pulled into regret, it is easy to lose perspective about being loved or being loveable at all. We are convinced that since we failed in the past we will never experience love again. It's as if we think we had our chance and blew it, so now there is no hope. But Hosea's words give us a whole new perspective. Not only is love available and freely offered to us, but God is actively pulling against the forces of regret to draw us out of our misery into a new life.

God's bungee cords of kindness and love pull us out of the mire of regret so that we can discover our life is not over. He is not finished with us yet. In the process, we find his love was there all the time, holding us and drawing us to himself.

8

Guilt

The Great Immobilizer

Go away from me Lord; I am a sinful man!

Peter (Luke 5:8)

uilt is like the air we breathe. It's constantly around us and within us, yet most of the time we are not aware of its presence or influence on us. Sales managers, teachers, ministers, and parents often use guilt in an attempt to motivate and push people to do better or accomplish more.

There is an assumption that if people are made aware of all they are doing wrong or how they have let others down, they will change their behavior and become better, more productive people.

How many times have I sat in church listening to a sermon that dumps guilt on the congregation? However, the congregation rarely rises up and responds to the guilt message by accomplishing "great things for God." More likely they sit quietly, thinking, *That's right, I blew it again. I don't have enough faith. . . . I should have done more.* Then they get in the car and drive home wondering what to eat for lunch.

Clint Eastwood won an Academy Award for his film *Unforgiven*. It's a bleak, raw, and violent portrayal of pain, guilt, and revenge. His character is an aging gunfighter hired by a group of prostitutes to avenge the abusive mutilation of their friend.

Clint teams up with a brash, big-talking teenager who wants to be a gunfighter too. In one gripping scene the kid murders one of the bad guys in an outhouse, then later processes the shooting with the older gunfighter.

At first he is bragging and talking tough, but soon he is overwhelmed with what he has done, killing a man for the first time. "He had it coming. . . . He had it coming, you know," he blubbers into his liquor. Then steely-eyed Clint responds, "We all have it coming."[1]

The truth of this observation is significant for all of us. We are guilty. Perhaps not of the things accusers throw our way, but deep down we know, "We all have it coming."

I'm not sure why, but it seems to me that we often marry someone who has a slightly different guilt barometer than we have. Years ago when I was in graduate school, Eileen and I were driving through Pasadena, and a cop who had been driving behind us suddenly turned on the red lights and pulled me over.

My immediate reaction was guilt. *What have I done now?* My mind flashed through a series of infractions: speeding, turn signals, tailgating, but I couldn't bring anything to mind.

The policeman came up to the car, asked a few questions, then indicated I could go on my way. I had to ask. "Wait, why did you pull me over?" He stared at me for a minute and replied, "I noticed you were driving very carefully, observing all the traffic laws impeccably, so I assumed you might be a drunk driver trying to cover it up. I just wanted to check it out. Have a nice day."

Suddenly my wife leaned over and announced, "He's innocent this time but you should give him a ticket for all the things he's gotten away with!" My own wife thinks I deserve a citation on general principles. And she's right, of course. The problem is not that we are innocent, but that we are guilty and we know it. What we don't need is other people reminding us of our guilt.

Our legal system may contribute to our being all mixed up about guilt and innocence. When a person is accused of a crime, they come before a judge and plead guilty or innocent. That seems fairly straightforward. But when the case comes to trial, the issue of guilt or innocence becomes very blurred.

Eileen was called to jury duty. It was a trial in which the young suspect, who was accused of stealing a car, had a long history of car thefts and was caught with a stolen car after being involved in a long, high-speed chase.

When the police were finally able to stop his car, he jumped out and fled, and they had to chase him until he was finally captured. It seemed to be a clear-cut case.

But his lawyer informed the jury, "This is not a question of innocence or guilt. The issue is, will we be able to present enough questions that you might be able to assume there could possibly be reasonable doubt? Then you don't have to convict him. Ladies and gentlemen of the jury, don't ask if he is innocent. Ask if there is perhaps reasonable doubt that might be established."

Herein lies a problem. According to our court system, guilt or innocence take on new meaning. But our lives, unlike a courtroom, are not about creating reasonable doubt. Rather, we can experience a godly sorrow that leads to repentance and freedom (see 2 Cor. 7:10). As long as we have to build a case for reasonable doubt, we are not free.

A Gift of Criticism

I had just finished speaking to nearly a thousand people at a conference and I felt great. I'd nailed it! Flush with a sense of victory, I left the platform and approached a group of attendees waiting to talk with me. The first person in line shook my hand and emphatically stated, "You said ex-cetera. That is wrong. You made a mistake. The word should have been pronounced et-cetera." I was stunned. My mind floundered around, trying to understand this crazy conversation.

He went on to tell me that he had been an English teacher and believed he had a gift for criticism. Then he offered to make me a deal. "This weekend I'll make a note of each verbal mistake, and then I'll come straight to you so I can correct your mistakes."

I was flabbergasted. Finally I responded, "No thanks, but you can make a note of anything I say correctly, any phrase that follows accepted sentence structure, and any word I pronounce correctly. Then come and tell me how I've done." He walked away disappointed; I was just glad he walked away.

My friend Bruce told me, "It takes ten 'atta-boys' to make up for one 'you jerk.'" Sometimes people find it easier to point out our failures than to celebrate what we've done right. It isn't surprising that we find ourselves in a toxic environment of spoken and unspoken judgment. Paul Tournier observed:

> I am speaking only as a psychologist and a man. I cannot study this very serious problem of guilt with you without raising the very obvious and tragic fact that religion—my own as well as that of all believers—can crush instead of liberate. There is a kind of unavoidable reverse side to every declaration of faith, which follows it as faithfully as shadow follows sunshine.[2]

Soon the weight of guilt (both real and imagined) pushes down on us until we find it difficult to live with freedom and joy. Our freedom and joy are two things that matter to us and to God. Jesus said, "I have told you this so that my joy may be in you and your joy would be complete" (John 15:11).

Motivate by Guilt?

I think there is a misconception that somehow we can motivate people by getting them to feel guilty. Fund-raisers, parents, and bosses have attempted to guilt people into action. Unfortunately for them it is a completely wrong strategy. My friend Art taught me an important lesson when I was trying to motivate people to get involved in a worthwhile project. He observed me prodding them to action by focusing on (and encouraging) feelings of guilt. "John, don't you know that guilt is the great immobilizer?" he said. "When someone feels guilty they

Our freedom and joy are two things that matter to us and to God.

grind to a stop, give less, pull out of involvements, and disengage from relationships." He went on to share the lessons he had learned as the executive director of World Concern, a global relief agency.

Faced with the daunting task of raising millions of dollars for relief emergencies such as the ravages of famine, war, and earthquakes, he discovered that people actually contributed less when the marketing communication was guilt-based. However, when the advertising communicated the very real need and assumed people were caring and wanted to be generous, there was always a sizeable jump in contributions.

That got me thinking about all the times in my own life when I felt guilty, and at those times I tended to pull back or disengage from the issue and the people involved. Perhaps it was self-protection, but it might have also been the subtle inhibition that comes over us when we feel we don't measure up.

Like a lot of people, at an early age I had memorized one Bible verse: John 3:16. "For God so loved the world that he gave his one and only Son, that whoever believes in him shall not perish but have eternal life." It makes sense to learn this one, because it speaks of God's motivation of love for the whole world, the gift of his Son, and eternal life for those who believe. It is no surprise that this great verse from the Bible is widely quoted and frequently shared among followers of Christ.

I wonder why so few of us bothered to memorize, share, or even discuss what comes next in that passage of Scripture. The next verse is equally meaningful and central to understanding God's attitude toward the world, and what our attitude toward the world might be as well. "For God did not send his Son into the world to condemn the world, but to save the world through him" (v. 17). In other words, Jesus was not trying to make us feel more guilt; he was focused on helping us live free from its burden.

Guilt We Deserve and Guilt We Don't Deserve

Guilty feelings in a person's life can take many subtle forms. Some of our guilt is obvious and well deserved. When we mess up publicly, or are found out for the mistakes or wrongs we have committed, guilt emerges and we recognize instantly why we have it and what we have done to get into this predicament. Other times guilt springs up and we are not aware of its cause. It is common for people to experience feelings of guilt without an understanding of its origin. Psychologists refer to guilt complexes and unconscious sources of guilt that can surface and affect us in many ways.

We also carry guilt not just for things we have done wrong, but also for things we didn't do that we believe we should have done. These "sins of omission" weigh us down because we could have taken action or spoken up or helped in some way, but we did not do it.

In the novel *The Kite Runner* by Khaled Hosseini, a young boy looks around a corner to see his best friend being molested by bullies. Thinking no one can see him, he watches the abuse in horror, until the victim's eyes meet his and they silently look at each other. Nothing is ever said of the incident, but the guilt for what he didn't do, for not intervening, weighs on him for years.

Forgiveness is the only antidote for our guilt. Of course I expect to be forgiven for offenses large and small that I commit. It is far more difficult to forgive those who have "sinned against me." We can find ourselves hiding behind a weak excuse, such as we'll forgive as soon as they come to their senses, recognize the horrific offense they perpetrated on us, and sincerely ask for our forgiveness (begging for it might be better). Of course while we hold out for this resolution that will probably never come, we remind ourselves that harboring resentment and reliving the pain are entitlements we deserve.

Even though we know that eventually we'll have to forgive people for the things they did (or didn't do) to us, forgiving can still be a difficult thing to do. In time we'll have to get around to forgiving them, but maybe hell would freeze over before that time came. In my own life, I could see that even as time passed, my anger didn't. I realized I couldn't be free to move on until I made the hard choice to forgive those who had hurt me deeply, but I was never quite ready to let go.

I had taken a red-eye flight from Seattle to Newark, where I was to make an early morning connection to my flight into Grand Rapids, Michigan. I had a forty-five-minute wait before the next flight was to take off. Sitting in the terminal, I looked over the notes for the talk I was scheduled to present at 10 a.m. in Grand Rapids. I knew there would be plenty of time to arrive, get a rental car, go to the hotel, shower, and change clothes to be ready for the presentation.

I was speaking on the power of forgiveness and I was confident of the message and my delivery. Everything was going well. But then our flight time came and went without an announcement from the airline. When I went to the counter and inquired, they assured me that nothing was wrong and we'd be boarding soon. I went back to my notes. My mind kept returning to the question, *When am I going to forgive the people I used to work with who hurt me?* My answer to myself was always the same: not now.

After a couple more hours and three different delay announcements, I had it worked out that I could still arrive in Grand Rapids and go straight to the engagement, skipping the hotel, shower, and fresh clothes, and still be on time for my presentation. We were then informed that the problem wasn't mechanical. Evidently they were missing a flight attendant for our plane, but they'd located one in Cincinnati who was being flown in and would arrive momentarily, and then we'd be on our way. No worries.

I phoned the folks in Michigan to let them know that we were having a slight issue, but not to worry if I was a few minutes late. Everything would work out fine. They were hesitant but hopeful. At last we boarded our little commuter plane and were ready to go, having witnessed the arrival of our brand-new Ohio flight attendant. I put the forgiveness issue to the back of my mind and boarded the plane, relieved to be on the way. Buckled in my seat on the tiny plane, I once more reviewed my notes and started to think about forgiving the folks who had wronged me. One by one these individuals I had once considered friends came into my mind. I realized that there would be no peace and certainly no freedom for me to get past the hurt until I released them, but I figured I'd wait until I got home to actually forgive them.

Just then the captain's voice came over the speaker informing us that there was a delay and we would be waiting out on the tarmac until clearance was given for our flight to take off. Three different times the captain updated us that we'd be going soon. I used my cell phone to call Grand Rapids and let them know I wouldn't be there for the presentation after all. We sat for another hour, and then I gave up.

Whispering, so my seatmates wouldn't be bothered, I told the Lord that I forgave them. Speaking each of their names, I released them one by one from the hurt they had inflicted on me and my family. When I was finished, I told the Lord that I would probably be coming back to do this a few more times, and I'd probably need divine help to put the whole terrible experience behind me. Just as I closed the prayer with a quiet "amen," the captain came over the speaker to announce we were cleared for takeoff. The engines roared and we soared off toward Michigan and the new beginning of my life.

I certainly don't want everything I deserve. I'll take grace any day.

I'm not saying that if you refuse to forgive those who have harmed you, God will trap you in New Jersey until you're ready to forgive. But I believe that is what happened to me. Imagine if I would have held on to my bitterness and refused to forgive. I might still be sitting in Newark.

Jesus, in what has come to be called the Lord's Prayer, makes it very clear that our experience of forgiveness is directly correlated with our extending forgiveness to those who have betrayed and hurt us. I don't believe any of us deserve forgiveness.

Those who have wounded you certainly don't deserve your forgiveness. Forgiveness is inseparably linked to grace. Grace is the gift of giving someone what they don't deserve. Perhaps the worst curse we could put on someone is that they would get what they deserve. I certainly don't want everything I deserve. I'll take grace any day.

When we find ourselves in uncharted waters of guilt and loss, it is not uncommon to also have great feelings of powerlessness. We find it hard to muster the energy to get out of bed, much less step out into a busy life. There can also be an overwhelming sense of disorientation, which leaves us feeling ineffective and unprepared for the future. Of course if we surmise there is no future, we can settle into a malaise of depression and hopelessness. The shadow of our own sense of guilt darkens our perspective as we accuse ourselves of bringing this on ourselves. Thinking we should have known, we should have acted, or we should not have done something can haunt those who find themselves disoriented in their own skin.

When I'm tempted to look back and mull over the worst moments in my life, there are the usual emotional knee-jerk reactions: sadness, resentment, guilt, anger, and frustration. But the primary hurt is the sense of shame that haunts me. Even though I can resent and brood about what was done to me, there is a deep sense that I probably got what I deserved. *After all,* I tell myself, *it was only a matter of time before others found out what I've known all along . . . I'm no good.* My self-incrimination has been cultivated over a lifetime. Rejections large and small accumulate in the shadows of my heart and mind.

Carol was stuck. Her husband who had abused and controlled her for so many years was dead. Sitting in my office, this intelligent, beautiful, widowed mom seemed unusually nervous and anxious. Suddenly she blurted out that she had met a man who, in spite of everything, seemed to love her, related well with her kids, and had indicated a desire to marry her. But instead of being excited, she was distraught.

As we explored her responses and resistance to moving further in this relationship, the wounds and shame from living in an abusive marriage began to surface. Then we saw what bothered her. "When I was married to Brad, it was as if the person who knew me best, who had been a central part of my life and who saw my flaws, fears, hopes, and secrets, constantly told me that I was unlovable," she said. "What if I let someone else in, and they get to know me that intimately—they will also discover what Brad knew—that I am really not loveable!"

There was shame, doing its best to accuse, threaten, judge, and condemn this marvelous person. After a minute of silence, I asked, "What if Brad was wrong? What if he didn't understand you at all and never saw your worth? Maybe he was stupid and selfish and made the biggest mistake of his life!" With a hint of a smile, Carol looked up and asked, "You think he might have been wrong about me?"

One aspect of shame's power is that it causes us to pull away from each other. Rather than moving toward people with grace and freedom, we cover up and hide behind a wall of pain-filled defensiveness.

Come Find Me

If the antidote for guilt is forgiveness, then the antidote for shame is inclusion. When we experience rejection, loss, and abandonment, the shame that slips in through the cracks of our brokenness reminds us we are unworthy of being loved. Thus the rejection we experience is doubly painful, because in our minds it turns out to be our own fault. If only we'd done something. If only we hadn't done something. If only we'd said something. If only we hadn't said something.

If the antidote for guilt is forgiveness, then the antidote for shame is inclusion.

It seems that when something good happens we attribute it to grace or God's blessing, but when bad things happen we assume we had it coming.

How do our feelings of guilt grow into an overwhelming sense of shame? How does it take hold in our heart and mind? Perhaps it begins with a small but crucial miscommunication. As children we heard well-meaning statements: be good, be strong, be smart, be quiet, and be perfect. These and other similar statements filtered into our thinking, and we interpreted them to mean something quite different from their original intent: "We will love you *if* you will be strong, good, and perfect." Since we all want to be loved, we determined that we would keep our part of the bargain, so we set out to earn the love for which we longed.

Unfortunately, we all blew it eventually. Despite our best efforts, we failed miserably. We weren't perfect, or good, or quiet, or whatever. Now (in our childish reasoning) we assume we can't be loved because we let them down. We feel guilty for falling from our lofty position of perfection and lovability. Then the first seeds of shame take root and begin to grow in the deep places of our soul.

In our fallen (unlovable) state of shame, we run away, cover up, or even try to hide from those who might have loved us. My kid sister Florence hid in the back of our closet, behind all the clothes and toys. I found my perfect hiding place: a huge pepper tree in the backyard. To me it looked like a weeping willow with long, wispy branches hanging down to the ground. I discovered that if I pushed my way past the wall of leafy branches there was a secret, sheltered area near the trunk where the world couldn't find me and I could sit and mull over the unfairness of life.

But even while we hunkered down in our secret places, we still longed for one thing: that someone would come find us. So I'd sit, listening for the sounds of concerned family or friends. I thought to myself, *When they notice how long I've been gone, they will be so sorry, they will come searching for me and when they find me—everything will be all right and I'll be loved once more.*

Of course, no one ever came for me. Eventually I'd make my way back to the house and determine that the next time I'd be perfect and then they would have no choice but to love me. Despite my good intentions, inevitably I'd fail again and the cycle of failing, hiding, recommitting, and failing again spiraled along throughout my life. This repeating pattern feeds our feelings of shame. Then shame is perpetuated by a deep-seated fear that we will inevitably mess up and be rejected all over again.

I got the message early on that whatever or whoever I was—it was wrong. The message in my church was, "God can't use someone like you." At school, it was, "Work harder and talk less or you'll never amount to anything." At home it was, "What is the matter with you?" With all my apparent dysfunction and quirky personality traits, I would have to become "someone else" before I had any chance of succeeding in this thing called life.

I identified with Woody Allen's quip, "My only regret in life is that I'm not someone else." So I tried to become someone else. I'd look around to see who was popular, effective, and well liked, then I'd try to act like them. This worked for a while because I was pretty good at pretending. And because I was fairly smart, I soon became adept at reading people and figuring out what they wanted or expected me to be. Then

I'd try to be the person they wanted me to be. But despite my best efforts, I would inevitably let them down. My true self would eventually emerge and soon they would see what others had surely seen before, that I wasn't perfect. In fact, I was quite flawed.

My friends and I talked a lot about the value of being vulnerable, authentic, and real. But we never got beyond the words and discussions. Vulnerability was reduced to sharing old issues or problems from the past that we'd already worked through. Our current struggles got buried someplace where we could keep them hidden.

Like a lot of people, I got pretty good at "faux intimacy." That is the sharing of things that sound vulnerable but are not. I remained distant and in control while appearing open and vulnerable. Of course faux intimacy can lead to highly manipulative, shallow relationships. Over and over I'd notice people would become frustrated, thinking we were in an authentic relationship but struggling to deal with the walls I used to keep them at a safe distance. I was in control of my short-term, shallow relationships, but the result was loneliness and wariness toward the very people who meant the most to me.

I began to realize that I had spent my life on the outside fringes of relationships. Maybe I reasoned that if I wasn't really relationally connected, then I couldn't really be rejected.

In high school I had learned about fooling people into thinking I belonged. I dreaded lunch hour, where it took about eight minutes to eat my sack lunch, leaving fifty-two minutes to stand around and pretend I belonged. Eventually I solved this loneliness dilemma by finding a group of classmates that I wished I was part of. I longed to belong and be included in their conversations, jokes, and camaraderie.

I would linger nearby, eating my lunch on the fringe of their friendship circle, then stand around and pretend to laugh, nod, and gesture as if I belonged to their group.

I knew I wasn't part of it, and they also knew I wasn't part of it. But sometimes other kids might suppose I actually belonged to that group of friends. I could get close enough to fool people into thinking I belonged even though I remained an outsider. I hid my fears and acted with great bravado. But I was still lonely and terribly afraid that someone would find out my secret and expose me as a fraud.

Looking back, I began to see that what I was seeking throughout my life was something with the power to free me from shame. Forgiveness is the antidote for guilt; now I needed the antidote for shame: inclusion. Like all of us, I wanted to belong. I wanted to be included, invited, and welcomed to join in. Feeling like an outsider not only feeds our loneliness, it cultivates our sense of shame.

It was about to be my first cold, wet winter. We left our home in Cardiff-by-the-Sea, California, to move up to Seattle and begin a new life and ministry at the University Presbyterian Church. Would we fit in? Would I be welcomed by the staff? Would I get along with the senior pastor, Bruce Larson? I had known him only through his books, although after about twenty books, I felt like I knew him a little bit.

Entering the foyer of the church for the first time, we saw a crowd gathering around Bruce, getting and giving hugs and words of greeting and encouragement. Eileen and I stood to the side, waiting nervously to meet the new boss. Suddenly he turned around, fixed his eyes on us, and smiled. He reached out and in the rich voice I would come to love, bellowed, "We've been waiting for you!"

126

That greeting, on that rainy December day, forever changed our lives and ministry. In one little sentence, he eased the burden of my shame and showed me what life could become. What had the power to overcome my shame? For the first time I, who was adept at standing on the outside of the circle, was included. It was as if he took a big piece of chalk and redrew the lines to include me. I was still me, still a mess of strengths and flaws and insecurities, but something was different. I was included. I belonged and shame couldn't hold me back any longer.

Years later, as Bruce lay dying, Eileen, Damian, and I gathered around his bed. "I'm going to heaven," he said. Then he grabbed Eileen's hand and said, "I'm in heaven right now."

When I get to heaven, I will probably be nervous, insecure, and wondering if I even belong there. I hope Bruce turns around, fixes his eyes on me, reaches out, and booms, "We've been waiting for you!" Then I'll know I'm home and I belong.

9

Anger

Getting Mad without Going Mad

Anger blooms in the absence of gratitude.

Don Colebourn

Dealing with anger has been a lifelong adventure for me. Anger, whether our own or others', impacts our lives in ways we don't always realize.

Physicians tell us that anger affects us physically. Our heart rate increases, pushing more oxygen-rich blood through our system, and blood even clots faster, thus protecting us in case of injury. It can also be a motivating tool for increasing achievement. Remember when Rocky had to get "the eye of the tiger" to win his match? Sometimes we need to get "fired up" for the challenges we face. Of course, anger also has a destructive side we are quite aware of. Unleashed anger can leave a path of destruction that would make tornadoes jealous. Countless relationships have been damaged and destroyed by inappropriate expressions of anger.

We need to explore the depths of our frustration when we are getting past our hurt. Shoving our anger down will not keep it from breaking out—at the worst times and sometimes in the worst ways.

In a counselor's office many years ago, I was shocked to hear her tell me she had never met anyone who was more out of touch with their feelings than I was. I didn't have a good response, because I knew something was wrong—my outer expressions and words were not connected to what was going on inside me. Cruel dictator Idi Amin has been quoted as saying, "Never confuse what I think with what I say." I could identify with that.

I'd studied enough psychology to be able to help many people work through their issues, yet I was a mess myself. Much of my life was spent on an emotional teeter-totter, balancing anger on one side and depression on the other. Back and forth I'd go: sad to mad to sad to mad. People close to me let me know they liked me better when I was depressed, because at least then I was quiet.

I didn't want to be a person out of touch with my feelings, and I certainly didn't plan to be that way. It was time to begin the adventure of discovering and connecting with the emotional part of me.

Our personality and physical appearance are influenced by our biological and sociological environments. So too are we influenced in our experience of expressing emotions. My early years were important times for me to learn what to feel and how to express it. Even as a little boy, I was learning how to manipulate others with emotions.

When I was young, our family packed up and moved to Africa, where my dad built a missionary hospital deep in the equatorial jungle. Since it was all I knew, I assumed that was what everyone who lives in Los Angeles did. Boy, was I wrong. As a six-year-old growing up in Africa, I wanted to be included. Sometimes my parents would host groups of medical workers and missionaries in our home and the "adult talk" would drag on late into the night.

There always came that moment when my parents said it was time for me to go to bed. And I would predictably do my best to persuade, cajole, argue, resist, and fight to stay with the adults. It was a losing battle. Ultimately my dad would pry my clinging fingers off the sofa legs and carry me, kicking and screaming, to my bed. There I would yell, cry, and even beg to be let back into the adult room, all of which predictably left me alone with a headache and exhaustion.

One dark night I tried a different strategy. After being carried to my room and plopped on my bed beneath the hanging mosquito nets, I got an idea. No more crying and yelling for me, no more demanding a seat with the adults. This time I lay in my bed quietly, then tiptoed down the hall toward the living room. When I poked my head around the corner, they all saw my young face watching them silently, with just a little tear rolling down my chubby cheek.

"What's wrong, Johnny?" My mom asked, obviously concerned for my well-being.

"I'm afraid," I stammered. "It's dark in my room." (Of course it was dark; the kerosene lamp had been blown out.) "I heard the drums in our village and thought I heard scary things."

Something unimaginable happened. I couldn't believe my good fortune. My mom scooted over on the sofa and invited me to climb up and rest my head on her lap. Oh yeah, I was back in the room!

That was the night I learned how powerful emotional expressions could be in helping me get my way. I also learned that if getting mad and getting sad didn't work, sometimes being afraid was greatly rewarded.

We've all learned life lessons that have shaped our emotional expressions and taught us what works to get us what we want. Of course, as we mature we gain new insights that change our ways of expressing those complex feelings churning below the surface.

As the years passed, I found that acting afraid didn't work so much anymore, so I went back to my old friends sad and mad. It wasn't long before I was out of touch with my genuine feeling of fear. Instead of addressing it, I'd respond in anger or depression until I didn't even feel fear anymore.

Feelings get buried. Uncertainty about our feelings, or the appropriateness of expressing them, often leads us to covering them up, ignoring them, or pushing them below the surface. But they always find ways of popping up.

My favorite game at Chuck E. Cheese's Pizza Parlor was Whac-A-Mole. There were many different holes on the table, and the toy "head" would suddenly spring up and we were supposed to knock it back down into the hole with a rubber mallet. Faster and faster it went, until we were hitting the empty holes and completely missing the one with the toy head.

What may seem like fun in the loud, raucous party atmosphere of the pizza parlor becomes quite frustrating in real life. As we stand guard over our emotions, ever vigilant to "knock them back down" when they surface unexpectedly, and as we go through the ups and downs of life, it can become increasingly difficult to keep them under control. When they do break through we aren't prepared for the overwhelming intensity of the feelings we experience.

Healthy Anger

The Bible tells us, "In your anger do not sin" (Eph. 4:26). This important advice shows us, first of all, that anger in itself is not wrong. Some people who have been raised in the church have the mistaken belief that being angry is a sin. They often carry a load of needless guilt for the feelings of anger that churn inside, and now they not only have unresolved anger issues but feelings of guilt as well. Not only is it possible to be angry without sinning, it is essential for our emotional and spiritual health.

> *Not only is it possible to be angry without sinning, it is essential for our emotional and spiritual health.*

Some people like to express their anger by getting it out in the open. We all know folks who are expressers. They blast away, letting everyone know how they feel while venting anger in all directions. The expresser often feels great afterward. They get a generous kick of adrenaline, "blow off steam," and focus the blame on others. Those of us who feel dumped on are left to process the wrath that has spewed forth, and are often left wondering what it was all about. Eventually some people start finding excuses to pull away from the expresser because it is too painful to maintain a relationship with them.

But to repress the feelings that well up inside us is equally harmful. Don't get me wrong here; I like being with repressors because they are often quiet and compliant, as well as hesitant to express themselves in pressure situations. They can come across as easygoing people who are not quickly upset. Of course they also can appear cold, unfeeling, and emotionally distant, which is not that much fun.

Fortunately, between expressing and repressing is another, healthier option: confessing our feelings. In confession we can freely acknowledge our situation and our emotion. We own the anger and share openly about its basis, intensity, and significance.

By confessing, we bring the emotion up out of the depths of our soul and honestly explore our intense feelings. Then we can see what contributed to our feeling this way, including who or what stirred up this strong emotion, and finally we can explore options for resolving the underlying issues.

It is always surprising when the anger flows. One minute we are just going along peacefully, when something happens. It's usually nothing big at first, but don't worry, it gets big really fast.

We are all different, so we respond differently to what's going on around us. What triggers an explosion in one person may not bother someone else at all. Perhaps that is why we find anger so confusing, frustrating, and sometimes frightening.

I can tolerate a lot and am pretty easygoing much of the time. But I know some of the things that can push me to anger. This may seem silly or not worth getting upset over, but here is one: I can't stand bullies. I also can't stand people who act like bullies. There. I've said it.

Perhaps it started where all things start—in the hallways of junior high school. Since I skipped a grade when I returned from Cameroon to enter the school system, I was a year younger than my classmates. I knew enough to do all right in class, but emotionally and physically I was always behind the growth curve. This meant I was bad at sports and couldn't compete on the playground or with the girls. I was a dweeb and didn't know why—I just knew I was a prime target for bullies.

Now, every kid gets a certain amount of teasing, mocking, shaming, and being pushed around. So I'm not saying I was alone in this, but I was scared and too afraid to tell anyone. I was hopeless that I'd ever get out of the living hell my life had become.

Cory was the worst. He would find me at lunchtime (hiding among a few dweeb friends) to threaten and intimidate me. Of course the old trick of standing on my shoes then pushing me so I'd fall back and hit my head on the pavement always got a big laugh.

But it was his big threat to meet me after school with his friends and beat the stew out of me that left me shaken. All through the day, I was sure that life as I knew it would soon end. In the halls between classes Cory's friends would run up to me just to make sure I hadn't forgotten what was in store. I hadn't forgotten.

When my last class was almost over, I pretended that I needed to go to the restroom. I never came back. It took me about five hours to get home that day. Hiding in alleys, skulking through yards, ducking behind cars, loitering in stores, I carefully threaded my way home—sure that any minute Cory's gang of bullies would find me and destroy my destiny.

No one asked where I'd been or why I was late. I didn't offer anything. I don't remember sleeping that night.

The next day in science class one of my friends started taunting me. I guess he thought by siding with the bullies he'd be safe. At one point he was throwing wadded up paper at my head, and I just sat there in silence, feeling ashamed and helpless. I was doomed.

The bell rang to signal the end of class, and I gathered my books and papers and headed out the door. But my friend wouldn't give up. As I stepped into the hallway he smacked me in the head with his science textbook.

Something snapped. I whirled around and punched my friend Ken right in the face. Then I stood there, hoping that would be the end of it, I guess. But I was wrong. He charged me like an angry bull. Suddenly we were punching and grappling and bouncing off lockers while dozens of kids stood around and watched in amazement.

The science teacher pounced on us and stopped the fight, for which I was eternally grateful. We were dragged off to the vice principal's office where we sat until our parents could be contacted and our punishment could be handed out. Of course the school authorities didn't care who started it, who was the bully, or even who (me) was an innocent, terrorized victim.

Both of us were suspended from school—not to return for two whole weeks. During that time we were to have no contact with the "good" kids of Horace Mann Junior High. Of course that meant the only people we could talk to were each other. So for two weeks we hung out like the friends we were and then reentered the school.

A miracle had occurred in my absence. Everywhere I went, students were pointing at me and whispering. In some bizarre junior high parallel reality I had become a kind of folk hero. I was the kid who was kicked out of school for fighting!

Even Cory started acting like we were old friends. I never had to fight again. But I still hate bullies.

Bullies thrive because they can. They grow strong by serving the poison of "What if?"

Psychiatrist Fritz Perls developed Gestalt therapy to help people face their fears and live lives free from the tyranny of "what if" and the victimization it brings. His encouragement to go toward our fear seems counterintuitive. Why in the world would I want to go toward what I fear? Naturally, I'd like to get as far away as fast as I can! But Dr. Perls was on to something. He understood that those things we hide, suppress, or flee from become an all-consuming part of our unconscious mind.

Paul admonishes the early Christians to, "having done all—stand" (Eph. 6:13). In another passage, while describing Satan as a roaring lion stalking us, does the Bible instruct us to faint in fear of his bullying behavior? Not at all. James 4:5 tells us, "Resist the devil and he will flee." Who is it that runs away? According to Scripture it is Satan himself, the father of all bullies.

When Jesus affirms Peter and his declaration of faith, he tells him that he has been given the keys to the kingdom, and upon him Christ would build his church. Then he makes the most unusual statement. He tells Peter, "The gates of Hades will not prevail against it" (Matt. 16:18). I'm coming to think this may be one of the most misunderstood and misapplied statements in all the Scriptures.

Through the years I have heard preachers invoke this passage to encourage their congregations that, though Satan's attacks seem relentless and hell is powerfully unleashed on earth, we will be safe and ultimately protected by Jesus. If what they say is true, all we need to do is stay sheltered by Jesus and our faith will keep the attacks of evil from harming us.

As we stand up against evil and bring God's light and love to the darkness of this world, even the gates of hell will not be able to hold us back.

But wait! Jesus isn't saying anything about our being attacked by evil, much less hell itself. Suddenly it hit me. How often have I been attacked by a gate? Not that often. Ok, never. How often have I had to seek shelter because a mean gate was trying to mess up my life? Never.

Jesus is not warning us of Satan's attacks. He is calling us to stand up to the king of bullies and invade his domain. The gates of hell are not intended to keep evil in—they are meant to keep God's kingdom out. So Jesus is saying that as we stand up against evil and bring God's light and love to the darkness of this world, even the gates of hell will not be able to hold us back.

Not all bullies use physical intimidation. Some use words to cut at a person's heart and erode their confidence. Some use ideas to argue others into submission. Some use their age, position in life, wealth, or influence to make others feel small and insignificant.

This kind of bullying is every bit as destructive as standing on someone's shoes and shoving them down on the playground. Evidently Timothy, Paul's associate and friend, was finding himself the victim of intimidation in the church. Paul writes to encourage him, saying, "Don't let people put you down because of your youth. God did not give us a spirit of timidity, but a spirit of power, love, and self-discipline" (see 2 Tim. 1:7).

Timothy could not run from the bullies in the church, nor did he have to resort to their destructive tactics in order to win their support. But Paul has an important insight about this kind of problem. He said, "Don't *let them*." Bullies thrive because we let them intimidate us, we let them look down on us, and we let them shame us. Paul's advice carries the message that we no longer need to consider ourselves victims. Jesus has given us a new spirit that is not based in shame and helplessness.

Getting Past Our Anger

I've never had a creative thought while angry. Certainly I've been focused, flummoxed, forceful, and even formidable—but creative? Not really.

When our bodies and minds experience anger, the feeling can be so intense that it is easy to understand why we might assume we are creative and effective in handling changes in our life. But don't trust self-perception. Our choices, decisions, and statements all look a little different when we calm down.

Getting past what we'll never get over will require new approaches, new options, new responses, and new outlooks. Our anger can stick us in emotional ruts from which we have difficulty getting out.

It is important to take the necessary steps to get past the negative impact of our own anger. This can be difficult because we often use different words to describe our experience of anger. We might consider ourselves to be frustrated, upset, or even passionate. Unfortunately it is quite possible to confuse anger with passionate feelings. This happens to me from time to time. I'll blow up about something and then try to reinterpret the incident by saying, "I'm not angry, I'm just being passionate!" Please believe me when I say that when someone says this, you can safely assume it is really anger and not just passion.

Sometimes when a person chooses to move beyond anger they are surprised to find a lack of support, even among their closest friends. I've had friends with whom I vented my feelings of anger and they in turn vented theirs. This was fine—until one of us changed the communication pattern and the others no longer knew how to respond appropriately. Friendships have become strained and sometimes ended because our unspoken agreement had changed.

It is possible for a culture of anger to pervade an office, home, church, or school. It becomes like the air we breathe: not always visible, yet ever present. Unresolved frustrations or resentments and relational scars that accumulate can fester below the surface, unacknowledged. Is it any wonder that at staff meetings or planning sessions there is very little positive creativity expressed? Plans for change and growth are met with lackluster response and even when approved might never come to fruition. Of course this is unnecessary. It is when we move past the anger barrier that we experience a burst of creativity and energy beyond our expectations.

How does this happen? It comes with practice. I've found that in the same way I have to practice playing my guitar, I also must practice thinking, speaking, and acting in non-angry ways.

I wish it weren't true. I'd love to just pick up the guitar and start playing like Jimi Hendrix. I even own the same kind of guitar that Jimi played: a Fender Stratocaster. It has the same number of strings, the same physical makeup, and potentially can make the same sounds. I imagine if Jimi were alive today and walked into my house, picked up my Strat (turned upside down for left-handed players), and started playing, it would sound incredible. But in my hands . . . not as good.

Similarly, it will take practice to learn how to relate in anger-free ways. Perhaps it won't feel natural right away. We may even be a bit clumsy at first, and like my guitar playing our attempts at a new way of relating will sound discordant or off-key sometimes. But every once in a while we'll get it right and there will be harmony.

Why is it that we practice things like music, art, dance, and golf but not something as important as communicating in our relationships? I have met quite a few folks (usually men) who put far more effort, time, attention, and practice into playing golf than they ever put into nurturing the people in their lives in non-angry ways. Even as I write this I'm feeling a little squirmy, realizing that in many ways it is true about me as well.

Am I ready to change? Can I get past the anger hurdle? Of course I can. If I'm going to write about this for others, I might as well practice what I preach. Where should I begin? Well, let me see . . . I'm aware enough to admit that I carry around a certain amount of frustration about how I think things ought to be—and how they really are. I could start by unpacking that piece of baggage and looking at each new experience as a fresh start rather than the "same old, same old" I have set in my mind.

Instead of looking for things to turn out the way they always do, I could practice looking for new results. I could

practice treating people as unique individuals who are fasci-
nating to get to know, instead of writing them off as boring
losers who are stuck in their dull lives. What will I do when
my old attitudes of frustration and anger start to surface? It
does no good to pretend they aren't there, but neither does
it help to let them intrude on my life.

I'm going to try something. When I start to sense these feelings stirring inside me, I'll greet them and remind them that
this isn't their time or place. Imagine greeting your feeling of
frustration as if it were an old friend, then gently but firmly
reminding it of the healthy boundaries you have established.
I can imagine myself driving along in my red car, when my
mind starts to focus on a past hurt or betrayal. Isn't it strange
how often these things creep into our thoughts while we are
driving along?

"Hey frustration, there you are again!" I could say. "It's
been awhile since you've come to visit. I know you have lots
of things for me to think about, but this is not the time, so
you'll have to leave now."

Therapists who practice behavior modification treatment
might recommend using a tangible, physical reminder such
as placing a rubber band around one of your wrists. Then
when the thoughts intrude into our minds we simply snap
the rubber band, literally telling ourselves to "snap out of it."

There are many different methods to cultivate new, creative ways of thinking, speaking, and relating. The particular
technique is not as important as the practice of consciously,
intentionally relating with others in situations where we previously acted out of habit, conditioning, or instinct.

When someone tells me that they are reaching the point
where anger is dominating their lives and they are feeling

more and more out of control, I work with them to realize that they can control it.

The first step is to consider, "How long do I need to be angry?" Each person might answer differently, but we all can think about our day and decide how much "anger time" we need. One man came to see me who felt as if he were constantly raging. When I asked him how long he needed to be angry, he responded, "I guess one hour in the morning and one hour at night would be enough." After we talked about this he agreed, as an experiment, to set aside two hours a day for two weeks to be totally angry.

I suggested during those two hours he could express his rage any way he wanted. Yelling into a pillow, singing along to really loud gangsta rap music, writing rage-spewing letters (not sending them), going out to a deserted place and screaming at the top of his lungs, fantasizing about all the terrible things he'd like to see happen to the people he's mad at, and much more. Then, after exactly sixty minutes, he would have to stop and go on with his life. If during other parts of the day the angry feelings started to emerge, he must tell them that they would have their time at the next appointed hour.

He shared with me later that after a few days some changes occurred. A couple of times it was hard for him to keep going for a full hour. After thirty or forty minutes he thought he'd done enough, but still had to make a half-hearted effort to fill the time. One day, he said, he completely forgot the morning session and only when it was time for the evening session did he realize he'd missed his "anger appointment." In time, the venomous letters morphed into journaling, and he no longer felt like driving out of town to yell in rage. After two weeks, we met to consider what had happened. This time when I asked, "How long do you need to be angry?" he paused for a second and with a smile said, "I think fifteen minutes a day should be enough."

What if you don't feel anger at all? Some of us who grew up in an environment that was intolerant of anger honestly can't identify the emotion inside us. When someone can't identify any angry experiences, I might ask, "What is frustrating you now?"

Because frustration is sometimes a more acceptable term, it can unleash a cascade of events or experiences that have frustrated us terribly. It isn't long before, if we're honest, we make the connection that those feelings of frustration are not so different from someone else's feelings of anger.

When the unfairness of life, the meanness of people, the pain of rejection, or the shock of tragedy threatens to overwhelm us, anger is God's gift for self-preservation. It can help us stand up and step forward toward our good future. But unconfessed, it can undermine our relationships, destroy our health, blind us to reality, and hold us back from living in freedom.

Madeline came to see me one afternoon. She was an elderly woman who I had been told was in the final stages of her battle with cancer. I was shocked when she sat down nervously and blurted out, "I'm here to apologize." I didn't have any idea what she was talking about. Then she told her story.

During her last examination, her doctor asked her an unexpected question: Was there anyone in her life toward whom she harbored such intense anger and resentment that she would rather die of cancer than resolve the situation? Immediately, she thought of me.

I was bewildered because we had never to my knowledge had an argument or disagreement in all the time we had known each other. She explained how some of her close friends had spread rumors about me and my family until her rage grew to the point where she was spreading lies and rumors as well.

"I know you probably could never forgive me for what I've done to you and your family, but I wanted to confess this before I die."

"Of course I forgive you," I told her, and we hugged while I prayed for her to be released from the grip of her destructive anger and find healing in her life.

When she left I sat in astonishment that I could be the object of such destructive rage and not even know it was going on. From that day, every time I saw Madeline we hugged and laughed and celebrated our relationship. When last I saw her she was still living a vibrant life, free from the crazy destructive grip of unconfessed anger, and her cancer was still in remission.

10

Bitterness

Drinking Poison and Waiting for Others to Die

> The first and often the only person to be healed by
> forgiveness is the person who does the forgiving.
>
> Lewis Smedes

My friend Sandy had patiently sat listening to me moan and groan while I rehashed an incident that had left me hurt and increasingly bitter. She was very patient as I went on and on about "those people" and what they deserved for their cruelty.

Finally she interrupted me by mentioning she had seen Carrie Fisher's one-woman show, *Wishful Drinking*, the night before. I didn't know what that had to do with anything but I pretended to be interested. Carrie Fisher had been Princess Leia in *Star Wars* so I guess she was entitled to do a one-woman show.

"In the show, she said that bitterness was like drinking poison and waiting for others to die. How long do you need to drink the poison, John?" She spoke with a smile on her face and a casual lilt in her voice, but I felt like she'd just smacked me across the head with a skillet.

Of course she was right. I was descending into bitterness. And I was only hurting myself by allowing the bitterness to take root. My brooding about pain, loss, and hurt were having no effect on those I resented. I pictured them having a wonderful time at a dinner party with friends, talking and laughing among themselves, while I was ruining our dinner by regaling my own friends with painful memories and seeping rage. How long did I need to drink the poison of bitterness? I determined that night it was time to quit cold turkey. The root of bitterness had to die before it killed me.

When resentment overlaps anger, often under a shroud of depression, bitterness starts to take over our lives. As it grows, our perception of reality can blur, our thinking can become distorted, and our ability to feel joy, love, or compassion can be blocked. In the same way that poison kills the body, bitterness kills the soul in a slow, very painful manner.

Martin Luther King Jr. had more grounds for bitterness than most of us, yet he saw the destructive nature of revenge. In his words:

> Darkness cannot drive out darkness; only light can do that. Hate cannot drive out hate; only love can do that. Hate multiplies hate, violence multiplies violence, and toughness multiplies toughness in a descending spiral of destruction.[1]

The feeling of bitterness is "so common and so deeply destructive," writes Shari Roan in the *Los Angeles Times*, "that some psychiatrists are urging it be identified as a mental illness under the name 'post-traumatic embitterment disorder.' . . . The disorder is modeled after post-traumatic stress disorder," she continues, "because it too is a response to a trauma that endures. People with PTSD are left fearful and anxious. Embittered people are left seething with revenge."[2]

When bitterness takes root in our hearts and minds, it is hard to pull up. The Bible refers to a "root of bitterness," which gives us a mental picture of the reality below the surface. I'm a terrible gardener, but I have done my share of weeding throughout my life. Weeds are tenacious not because of the growth we see above the ground but because of the growth below the ground that we don't see.

Roots grow in the soil, continuously deepening and expanding the weed's reach. It can be difficult to uproot weeds because too often their roots break off, leaving them in the soil to grow once more. There can be a similar dynamic taking place below the surface of our lives. Our hurt or resentment might not be visible on the outside, but under the surface bitterness is taking root, expanding its hold on our soul. Superficial attempts to rid ourselves of bitterness may result in a good appearance on the surface, but it sprouts back up quickly because the roots have taken hold.

I'm sure there are some people who love gardening, and maybe some even find weeding to be relaxing and enjoyable. Of course, I'm not one of them. Weeding to me always seemed like a big hassle. On those rare occasions I have "helped" in the garden, I wanted to do something meaningful like planting a flower, but instead I was usually relegated to weed patrol. I tried my best; I used my bare hands, a small spade, a rake, even a plastering trowel I found in the garage. Eventually

I moved on to a shovel and a pitchfork. If the ground was hard, I tried soaking it for a few hours to soften things up. I realize in hindsight that my efforts made no real difference. The weeds kept returning and I barely slowed things down. I suspect my family put me on weed patrol not to help the garden but merely to keep me occupied and out of the way.

Then a miracle happened. Someone invented Roundup. Roundup works because it mysteriously gets down deep and kills the roots of the weed. Think of it . . . no more clawing, pulling, and straining to pull up weeds by hand. Just spray a little and walk away—soon the weeds will die!

If only we could find a Roundup for our hearts and minds. Since most of our sincere attempts to dig out the roots of bitterness have been futile, we need something strong enough to counter the insidious root of bitterness. On the surface we may appear to be bitterness-free, but it is growing below the surface, taking control and destroying our lives.

Roundup for Our Soul

There is an antidote to the poison of bitterness. It makes its way deep into the decay of our soul and stops the negative power of our rage and resentment, releasing us from the never-ending cycle of despair and hopelessness. It is called grace. Grace demonstrated in forgiveness is the cure for bitterness and the means for getting past what we'll never get over.

When we choose to forgive those who hurt us, it isn't because they deserve forgiveness. Actually, they probably deserve the revenge we've thought about for so long. Grace is the gift of giving a person what they don't have coming. Grace is also the source of strength that provides us with the courage to let go and move on. The toxic poison of bitterness weakens us, but grace infuses us with strength to forgive and move forward to a new beginning where we can once again allow ourselves to give and receive love. Until we let go, we are not free to move forward with hope and joy.

Grace demonstrated in forgiveness is the cure for bitterness and the means for getting past what we'll never get over.

No one can force us to forgive. It is our choice alone, and it requires courage to face the wounds inflicted by others and release them from the prison of our own minds. "Suppose you never forgive," writes Lewis Smedes,

> suppose you feel the hurt each time your memory lights on the people who did you wrong. And suppose you have a compulsion to think of them constantly. You have become a prisoner of your past pain; you are locked into a torture chamber of your own making. Time should have left your pain behind; but you keep it alive to let it flay you over and over.
>
> The only way to heal the pain that will not heal itself is to forgive the person who hurt you. Forgiving stops the reruns of pain. . . . When you release the wrongdoer from the wrong, you cut a malignant tumor out of your inner life. You set a prisoner free, but you discover that the real prisoner was yourself.[3]

Victim Mentality

First of all, let's just admit we all feel like victims from time to time. We have received the assaults, survived the abuse, and absorbed the blows that come to everyone who lives and loves in this life. A victim mentality emerges when we lose perspective about our own responsibility for our feelings and for our actions in resolving the hurts we've experienced.

An honest look at those bruises we've collected at the hands of those "who care about us" is vitally important. Acknowledging the sometimes-harsh reality of our situations and relationships opens the door to a variety of choices we can freely make that will determine to a great extent how we move past what we'll never get over.

We must recognize that our victimization can be healthy when it leads us forward toward strength, healing, and new life. It also can become debilitating for us if we focus so much on the wrongs others have done to us that we let ourselves swirl down into a pit of regret, rage, and unresolved pain. The danger lies in our developing a victim mentality as a means for coping with pain and loss. Our attention begins to turn inward and we lose sight of our personal resources to live lives of confidence and hope.

Jeff is a man I've known for many years. He is intelligent, talented, well read, and at one time was fun to be around. He is fluent in three languages, yet rarely speaks to anyone anymore. You see, he was a victim of abuse early in his life. Those incidents have so consumed him that he never grew beyond it. It's almost like he remains a child in his mind, brooding and lamenting his childhood suffering. When people come into his life, they don't last there long. His wariness that they too might hurt him leads him to push people away to the point that he lives in a virtually isolated world of fantasy, regret, and bitterness.

The last time I visited Jeff, he was retelling the story of abuse. Then he looked over at me, and through pain-filled eyes said, "They took my life from me."

Thinking about it later, I realized that in a way he was right. They did take his life so many years ago. To a person with a victim mentality that is true to the core of their being. However, what we may never see is that all along the way there are choices we could make that could reduce our pain to a mere footnote in a life full of meaning and joy. But too often we don't allow ourselves to choose life.

In the Bible, Jonah could be considered "the bitter prophet." When I was a kid, I knew only about Jonah and the whale, which was the story we were told in Sunday school. Now as an adult, I get to read the rest of the story. In it I find a man who is consumed with bitterness. He didn't want to go and help the people who were facing impending doom. He hoped they would get what they had coming.

Bitterness has difficulty with grace. We don't want people to receive mercy when they deserve destruction. Jonah let his bitterness seep out and poison his whole worldview. He was angry with God, because he knew that God was forgiving and loving and would be merciful to the undeserving people.

At one point Jonah lashed out at God, saying in effect, "I knew it! I knew you were going to love. That's why I wanted nothing to do with this whole caper. That's why, back when I was at home minding my own business, and you said, 'Go to Nineveh and prophesy,' I said no! Because I knew you'd pull some trick like this and love them. And I can't stand it. Why can't you be judgmental? Why can't you blast them like I said you would? Why do you have to be so gracious, merciful, slow to anger, and abounding in love? What's the matter with you, God?"

I think Jonah represents someone who, no matter how good God is to them or what forgiveness God has brought to their life, and no matter how they have experienced grace, can't accept it for someone else.

I can relate to Jonah and even sympathize with him and his bitter attitude. I too have bitterness inside me. I keep it in check most of the time, but every once in a while it oozes out and I too want "them" to hurt and get what they deserve. I want them to suffer without mercy. But God asks, *Shouldn't I care? Shouldn't I show mercy to these people who are destructive and hurtful and mixed up?*

The whole issue of judgment is a tough one for me. I wrestle with the idea of God judging us, and I don't appreciate other people judging me either. Of course I tend to be blind to my own judgmental attitudes and statements because they come from me. I guess I do have a double standard that may contribute to keeping my bitterness alive deep inside me.

Jonah had a double standard. Although he was perhaps the most defiant and willfully disobedient of all the prophets in the Bible, he was least able to appreciate the forgiveness offered to the people he served. His pride stood in the way and blocked him from seeing the truth about himself, God, and the people. Pride is a dangerous thing, for it blinds us to reality and keeps us imprisoned in a false perception of the world. Humility, on the other hand, is the ability to see ourselves as the same as others: we are no different.

Gaining a Fresh Perspective

Protecting ourselves from developing a victim mentality is essential in order to move on in our life. It begins with preparing our mind. A false sense of security and safety is an open door for victimization. Mental and spiritual vigilance helps us avoid or maneuver through obstacles and threats.

Practice looking for options. There are always choices. We are not without options. Some may seem worse than others, but when we cultivate an option-seeking mindset we free ourselves to look for alternative ways to respond in any circumstance.

When we are in pain it is easy to lose perspective. The immediacy of our suffering and the intensity of our circumstances can keep us from seeing the bigger picture. This is why it is so important to cultivate a sense of perspective. Artists are often adept at visualizing perspective. But we don't have to be gifted artists to practice a "long look." Perspective in art is the visual relationship between seemingly disconnected objects. Breaking through the barrier of victim mentality begins with seeing our pain in a larger context.

Perspective increases when we share with others who have experienced similar loss. When we talk with someone who is further along the path of recovery, it encourages us to move forward with hope that things will not always be how they seem right now. Likewise, when we share from our experience with those whose lives have been recently shattered, it not only encourages them but helps us gain perspective by realizing how far we've come.

When my friend Darrel went through treatment for a brain tumor, our friendship grew deeper. To relieve his caregivers and his wife Diane, I would regularly spend the day with him, talking, walking, laughing, and sometimes reflecting on our lives. One time we were up in the town of LaConner, Washington, wandering through little art shops and antique stores. As we were eating our ice cream cones, Darrel smiled and said, "We need to build a wall with our memories. We owe it to ourselves to build good memories; at some point it may be all we have."

That sounded a little odd at the time, but it led to a good conversation about how to use our memories for good and not be dragged down by the painful ones. Darrel suggested that we consider good memories as building blocks, like the ones we played with as children. We could collect the good memories and use them to build a mental wall to protect us from the painful memories. He reminded me that I had allowed my painful memories to so dominate my mind and viewpoint that my good memories had all but disappeared from view. He was right. I began to realize that it was so much easier to remember the hurts and losses I had experienced. I rarely talked about or even considered the many good memories tucked away in some dark corner of my mind. The next day Darrel sent me a poem.

Build a Wall

Collect and build memories today
Like a child, with building blocks.
Memories that build hope in you and others.
Look people in the eye, smile with your eyes
Share thoughts, prayers, that grow, enrich
Give tokens of love—building blocks. Pile them up.

Build a wall with good memories,
Relish the ones you have.
I found a card from our 10th anniversary:
Build a wall that keeps the past behind
Hope looks forward
Faith steps forward
Love reaches out,
Reach out today
Someone will remember it.[4]

Right away I went to work on my new "Darrel Project." I felt like a kid on a treasure hunt. There was buried treasure to be uncovered and brought into the light—building blocks of good memories to dig up, brush off, and put into the memory wall I was building. At first I couldn't find very many, but as I searched through my mind, they began to bubble up to the surface one after another: a tender conversation with a friend, a celebrative moment, a note of gratitude, meaningful connections with people, counseling sessions, dinner parties, golf games, casual conversations in the hallway, or intense times with someone in the hospital.

I realized that for years I had kept a collection of letters from angry, unhappy people who were upset about something or other and had vented their rage on me. Where was my file of letters of appreciation, affirmation, and love? I had tossed those in the trash and kept the vitriolic ones for posterity. How mixed up was that? I grabbed the file of hate mail and dumped it in the wastebasket. Then I got a fresh file folder and labeled it "affirmations." I should have done this years ago.

Now when I get a letter from an unhappy person, I send them a polite response and toss their letter in the trash. When an affirmation arrives, I write a note of appreciation and put their letter in my file. I'm starting to build a wall of good memories, thanks to Darrel.

Freedom to Receive

The toxins released in our hearts and minds from bitterness often shut down our ability to be open and receptive to the many blessings and joys all around us. The lethal combination of resentment, rage, and despair can even keep us from recognizing and receiving the grace and love that are available to us. If we identify the issue and begin to understand why it is difficult for us to receive, we open ourselves up to being loved regardless of our circumstances, struggles, losses, or personal successes and failures. When we are loved regardless we become free to be our authentic selves without pretense or shame. In turn we can choose to love others regardless.

The toxic nature of bitterness can affect our souls in the same way poisonous toxins can affect our bodies. When Chris McCandless hitchhiked to Alaska in order to get back to nature, he didn't expect to be dead within a few months. His story was documented in the book *Into the Wild* by Jon Krakauer, which was later made into a movie. Evidently young Chris died from eating a toxic plant. The plant contained the same poison found in what ranchers know as locoweed. According to a paper published in the *Journal of the American Veterinary Medicine Association*, some of the signs of locoweed poisoning are "depression, a slow staggering gait . . . dull eyes with a staring look, emaciation, muscular incoordination, and nervousness (especially when stressed). In addition, affected animals may become solitary and hard to handle."[5]

When I read that, it struck me that these are also some of the symptoms we experience when we are being poisoned by bitterness. I wanted to understand more about how poison affects our bodily functions, since Chris wasn't killed instantly. Krakauer explained that the toxic plant rarely kills outright.

The toxin does the deed insidiously, indirectly, by inhibiting an enzyme essential to [our] metabolism. It creates a massive vapor lock, as it were, in mammalian fuel lines: the body is prevented from turning what it eats into a source of usable energy. If you ingest too much swainsonine, you are bound to starve, no matter how much food you put into your stomach.[6]

The poison Chris consumed from the toxic plant didn't kill him outright. But slowly, over time, it kept him from receiving nourishment from other foods. Because his ability to receive nourishment was blocked, he starved to death all alone in the Alaskan wilderness.

When we drink the poison of bitterness, a similar fate awaits us. The toxic nature of our resentment and rage effectively blocks our soul's ability to be nourished. Instead of growing stronger and healthier in our spirit and emotions, we actually start to resemble poor cattle that have feasted on locoweed: depressed, dull, jittery, stressed, and solitary. What a lonely, painful death it is for our souls. We spiritually and emotionally starve to death no matter how much "soul food" we are devouring. This helps us understand why so many bitter people may be active in church— reading the Bible, praying, studying, and striving to grow spiritually—yet are slowly dying inside. Bitterness blocks us from benefiting from the spiritual food we consume, leaving us weak and empty. When I consider some of those blocks, there are four that come to mind.

The toxic nature of our resentment and rage effectively blocks our soul's ability to be nourished.

One, it is a simple reality that in a world where relationships are often bartered, we don't want to owe. We don't want to be indebted. We don't want to have to pay back, so in our bitterness we tell ourselves its better not to receive, because we are going to owe. There is always a bill in a world where "the price is right."

Like most people, I get plenty of sales pitches on the phone. These are the people who call up and offer stuff that is too good to be true. These sales calls often have an absolutely free offer for us with coupons and free things and lots of bargains. "And best of all," they say, "it won't cost you a penny! Can I sign you up?" Sometimes I'll respond by saying I don't want to give them any of my credit card information, but they are certainly welcome to just send the free things to me.

Inevitably they explain that they can send me the free bargain only if I give them a credit card number. But wait—why do they need a credit card, if this is absolutely free? Then about three months later, buried on my credit card bill, is a hundred-dollar registration fee. Ouch. I thought I was receiving a gift, and now I have to pay. This can happen in our relationships as well.

There is a difference between healthy relationships with mutual expectations and manipulative ones that are exploitative. I sometimes get skeptical about people who initially seem overly friendly and loving, because I suspect more will be expected from me. If we get into a relationship that's honest, authentic, and loving there may be times that we call on each other, but too often it seems more like a scene from *The Godfather*, where the Godfather agrees to do a favor for someone, but then says, "Some day, and that day may never come, I will call upon you to do a service for me. But until that day, consider this justice a gift on my daughter's wedding day."[7]

I'm not saying that Jesus is like Don Corleone, or Marlon Brando for that matter. However the Bible tells us that to whom much is given, much is required (see Luke 12:48). It is perhaps natural for us to put up defenses in an attempt to keep from feeling overwhelmed by our spiritual and emotional debts. We can become indebted to God's love, for example. Paul identified himself as a "slave" for Christ. I'd be lying to you if I said God doesn't expect anything of us. He expects a lot from us. As he pours his love into us, he invites us to love in return, and to extend that love outward.

He gives us his gift of forgiveness over and over again, and he expects us to forgive the people around us. He also expects us to forgive ourselves; we owe him that. As we let him into our life, for example, he may help us grow strong and courageous, perhaps a little bolder. He might then expect us to come alongside other people and help them be courageous. To do in others' lives what God has done in our life, that is our debt. So we might think it's easier not to let God love us. It might seem easier not to let God forgive us and not to let God get close, because then we won't have to worry about what might be expected from us. But in fact, when we keep a balance between nurturing and being nurtured, we are not emotionally overburdened. Rather, we relate to others in healthy ways and resist the urge to attach strings and obligations to others.

Two, our bitterness also blocks us from receiving because we think, deep inside, we really don't deserve it. We don't deserve to be loved. Many of us have heard the message from our earliest days: "No one wants to hear from you. No one cares what you think."

I remember a little Sunday school lesson from my childhood. It went like this: "J.O.Y. equals Jesus, then Others, then You." Perhaps it could have been a helpful acronym, if it wasn't taught in such a stern way that the message I received very clearly was *you don't count.* Apparently, I was not as worthy of love as others. Jesus was worthy of love. Others were worthy of love. But not necessarily me. And unfortunately, too often we've taken that message to heart and think, *I can't receive blessings from God because I don't have it coming. I should do more to earn it.* Well—you can't do more. There is nothing we can do to get God to love us one bit more than he does right now. However, I don't think there is anything we can do to get God to love us one bit *less* than he does right now, either.

But like Wayne and Garth in *Wayne's World,* meeting the great rocker Alice Cooper, we say, "We're not worthy, we're not worthy."[8] Of course that is true. We're not worthy. None of us are worthy. Worthiness is not the point. Worthiness has nothing to do with it. That's why God sits back and says, *Yes, you are not worthy. Now will you let me love you anyway?*

Three, the poison of bitterness blocks us from receiving nourishment not because we think we don't deserve it, but because we think we deserve more. That's the flipside of feeling unworthy: *I deserve something different and better than this life. I deserve more than this share. I want a bigger piece of the pie. I'll hold out for a better option.*

At first, this sounds confident and almost arrogant, but it actually comes from the same self-doubt and insecurity as the "I don't deserve this" mentality. Some people hold back out of insecurity because they think they don't deserve any, but others hold back because they think they deserve more. The same lack of love for ourselves comes out in these two responses.

Four, sadly, we also miss out on many blessings simply because this is not what we were looking for, or this is not the way we imagined things would be. As I sat in the counselor's office, feeling exasperated, I was surprised when he told me that one of my counterproductive habits (that's the way counselors often speak) was that I would form pictures in my mind about how things were supposed to be, how I expected people to respond to me, and even how I presumed life will work out. Then, he said, I'd have experiences that I would continually hold up to my ideal and make comparisons. They seldom matched. Thus, I'd be frustrated that people let me down and life wasn't the way it should be. I was experiencing an almost constant state of disappointment because life didn't measure up to my mental snapshots.

It is difficult to receive when we are thinking, *This is not the way I planned it. This is not the way I'd hoped it would be. This is not the life I really intended to have. I want something else.* So we keep our options open and look past the good things that are all around us—and end up missing out on all the good things that don't line up with our preconceived ideas. We look past the good things because we are looking and waiting for something else.

Just Too Full

In the same way Chris's body was starving because the poison blocked any food from nourishing his body, our poison of bitterness weakens us by giving us the impression that we are full and don't need to be nourished. We live full lives with full schedules, full commitments, full bellies, and full social calendars. Thus, we think we have no room for anything else.

Imagine walking out of a restaurant having just finished a fabulous meal with friends. As you are about to drive off, your phone rings and it is someone inviting you to share a great meal—right now! They tell you about a wonderful place that serves fantastic prime rib with baked potatoes, fresh, warm sourdough bread, and a long salad bar that has every possible combination for you to pile on your plate. And don't forget the "death by chocolate" dessert that truly is to die for.

You tell your friend thanks but no thanks; you just don't feel like going out to eat right now. Then they think you're sick, or maybe you're mad at them since you would normally have enthusiastically jumped at the chance. Finally you reluctantly admit, "I'm just full."

Isn't this the way we are in many areas of our life? God wants to bless us with love, wisdom, and care, but we say no. *I don't feel like it. I'm full. My schedule is packed; there are responsibilities at home, school, work, and church. There is so much on my plate; I don't have the time or energy for one more thing. I'm full.*

Emotional overload also takes a toll. Even when we want to become involved with people and issues in our world in compassionate ways, we think we can't take one more thing. We are full emotionally, so we don't want to care more or get involved in other people's lives. We are cared out.

Sometimes I feel like that: cared out. It doesn't mean I'm uncaring; it's that my capacity to care has reached its limit. Face it: our lives are full. We laugh, cry, get depressed, get angry, get happy, celebrate, and get nervous . . . all these and more. There is so much swirling around us that we can't receive one more thing.

Besides our full commitments, our full minds, and our full emotions, I would suggest that our hands are full as well. I can't helpfully reach out to someone or invest in their life because my hands are so full, I'm afraid I'll start dropping stuff. How can I embrace someone when my hands are full? The fact is that before we can take hold of our new life, we have to let go of some things that we're holding on to. We have to set them down so that we have open hands, open arms, open minds, open hearts, and open schedules. We have to set things aside and create room to receive the love and strength to carry us forward.

> *We have to set things aside and create room to receive the love and strength to carry us forward.*

Bitterness, with all its resentment and rage, could be the first thing we choose to let go. It involves releasing those who hurt us from our emotional revenge list. In the movie *Billy Madison*, Adam Sandler plays the part of Billy, a young man who, in order to receive his inheritance, must return to his childhood schools and redo his dissipated past by succeeding in each grade level.

In a moment of clarity, he realizes that he and his friends had cruelly tormented a fellow student with childish pranks and teasing. Wanting to make amends, he calls the victim of their torment, Danny (Steve Buscemi), and apologizes for the harmful behavior when they had been in school together.

Danny quietly assures Billy that everything is forgiven, and he need not worry. Relieved to have made the call and apologized, Billy hangs up the phone—while Danny turns to a chart on his bedroom wall titled "People to Kill!" With a smile, he crosses Billy Madison's name off the list.

This bit of dark humor reminds me of the destructive power of our bitterness. While we long for revenge, or at least justice, we are the ones imprisoned in a cell of hate that we have built ourselves. Only letting go of the need to punish will free us to get on with life in healthy ways.

When he was finally released from almost thirty years in a South African prison, Nelson Mandela had good reason to feel bitter toward everyone who robbed him of a life of freedom for so many years, and everyone would have understood. However, Mandela saw forgiveness as the only way for him to move forward. He shocked the world when it was announced that he had invited opponents and even his jailor from prison to attend his presidential inauguration.

> I knew as well as I knew anything that the oppressor must be liberated just as surely as the oppressed. A man who takes away another man's freedom is a prisoner of hatred; he is locked behind the bars of prejudice and narrow-mindedness. I am not truly free if I am taking away someone else's freedom, just as surely as I am not free when my freedom is taken away from me. The oppressed and the oppressor alike are robbed of their humanity.[9]

Mandela knew from painful experience that, though released from prison, he would remain a prisoner of hate unless he forgave and released the people who caused him such suffering.

We will never be able to get past our suffering until we are willing to set the prisoner free. As we let go of bitterness that has sunk its poisonous roots into our soul and choose to forgive, we find the strength to take the first steps out of emotional prison toward the light of our new life.

11

Life's Unfair—What Will We Do about It?

There's been a misunderstanding, I thought when I saw the phone message on my desk. *That can't be right. I'll call back right now, and figure this out.* I had recently met Louise and liked her from the beginning. She was a single mom, raising a son and a daughter while teaching at a local high school. She radiated energy and creativity. I got to know her parents when I played with them on a local bowling team.

Sitting at my desk listening to the phone ring at her parents' home, I wondered what was going on. Verna, Louise's mother, answered the phone with a weak "Hello." I knew when I heard her voice that there had been no misunderstanding. Life for this family would never be the same.

Eileen and I later sat with the elderly couple in silence. What could we possibly say? Louise's father told us how the police had gone to Louise's house when she hadn't shown up to work and hadn't answered the phone all day. The police arrived at her house and quickly followed a trail of blood to the two-car garage, where they found Louise. Her dismembered body had been stuffed into the trunk of her car. Someone had murdered this loving and faithful mother in the most horrendous manner possible.

Gruesome as this was, there lay one more shocking discovery. Back in the house, covered with blood, Louise's son Bobby sat unresponsive and silent in his room. Bobby had killed and dismembered his mother the day before.

Her parents were overwhelmed by grief. We sat together quietly. At one point, Louise's dad whispered, "We've lost our daughter and our grandson too. We loved them both. How do we live now?" As I looked into the lost eyes of Louise's father, I saw a pain that could not be overcome. No one had to say it, but they would never get over it.

Three days later I stood in our church and led Louise's memorial service. Joining family and friends were hundreds of students from Bobby's high school, where she had taught. Each student came to honor her and try to understand the senseless murder and mutilation. I listened to the words of loving appreciation woven through the stories they told. Louise had nurtured and challenged these students to live with joy and vitality. It was very inspiring. Yet when it was over, I was suddenly overwhelmed by the unfairness of life.

Shaky Security

We tell ourselves that we are safe in this life, and that's a lie. When do we first convince ourselves that bad things don't happen to people like us? Living our lives in denial may not be very exciting, but it helps us feel safe. At least that is what we tell ourselves. But in settling for an imagined sense of security and safety, we lose our capacity to take risks and experience life as the adventure it was meant to be.

When my parents moved our family to Africa to serve in a mission outpost deep in the jungle, we weren't sure what we were in for. Living in the equatorial jungles of West Africa in my early childhood, I always looked out for a number of very real dangers. I practiced jumping over the trails of giant driver ants in the jungle that could devour a carcass in minutes. I kept a watchful eye for pythons in the low-hanging tree branches, poisonous insects in the foliage, hippos in the river, and lepers in our village. All of these everyday threats to my life and well-being gave me a wide-eyed suspicion of my environment and a pretty good sense of my vulnerability in the face of jungle realities.

In settling for an imagined sense of security and safety, we lose our capacity to take risks and experience life as the adventure it was meant to be.

Returning to the States and settling in the quiet town of Whittier, California, was a shock to my young worldview. Walking to Bethany Baptist Elementary School gave me a chance to be ever vigilant as I stayed alert for hidden pits of quicksand, rogue apes, or any other potential dangers lurking around me. Eventually I began to adjust to my new surroundings. My mental preparedness for potential harms and threats faded away, and before too long I began to feel safe. Life was apparently benign and the dangers were all in my young head.

Unfortunately I was completely wrong. Really, by moving from the jungle to the suburbs I merely traded one set of threats for another. Subtle deception, manipulations, cruelty, and the incredible vastness of human selfishness took the place of highly visible dangers in the jungles of West Africa.

I really liked my friend Billy's mom and dad. To me they were the perfect parents, and I would have gladly traded families with Billy in an instant. Only years later did I realize Billy's dad, a Ward Cleaver double, was stealing my valuable collection of first-edition uncanceled sheets of stamps from Cameroon. I believed him when he told me the cheap, canceled US stamps were a good trade. Of course I believed him; a dad like him wouldn't lie and cheat his son's best friend.

One day Jimmy, another neighbor kid, took a two-by-four and beat my pet Chinese pheasant Henry to death. I was shocked. Henry had followed me around the yard like a dog with bright feathers. My folks, oddly, took Henry to the taxidermist and had him stuffed for my tenth birthday present. I kept Henry mounted on the wall on my side of the bedroom, but the sadness stayed for a long time. Why would Jimmy do this to my Henry? Why would Billy's dad cheat me? Why would my Sunday school teacher desert his wife and four kids to have an affair with the young associate pastor's wife?

Eventually I came to accept that life is not fair. But I was ill-equipped to deal with the disappointing realities of suburban life all around me. It made me think that Africa might have been safer.

I do remember one place I could go where I felt safe and secure: the Jungle Cruise ride at Disneyland. After waiting in line expectantly, I would step into the boat and our guide would steer us out into a tropical river and into the deep jungle, all of which reminded me of Africa. This time, though, the animals were robots, the villagers had painted smiles on their faces, and the guide told the same jokes over and over, and never missed when he shot his pistol at the "dangerous" hippo rising out of the water wiggling his big ears. "Don't worry," our guide would say, "they are only dangerous if they wiggle their ears." I'd laugh nervously with the other tourists. Not even the waterfall could drench our boat. We were safe from all harm amidst the appearance of possible danger. I could have ridden that boat all day. But the Jungle Cruise was not the real world. It wasn't Africa and it wasn't Southern California either.

Perhaps we learn to surround ourselves with fantasies and diversions like the Jungle Cruise to convince ourselves that we are safe—nothing can hurt us. However, it shouldn't be surprising when we are then startled, shocked, dismayed, and bewildered by unexpected pains, losses, and regrets. Our safe, predictable lives are actually quite fragile, and like Humpty Dumpty on his wall, it doesn't take much of a push to leave us so broken it feels like we'll never be together again. In those times I'm tempted to cover up and protect myself from the wear and tear of living.

Building Calluses

When we are in pain, the longing for protection is irresistible. Sometimes we become callused in an effort to protect ourselves from further hurt. I have personal experience with calluses. One winter I decided it was time to start having real, roaring wood fires in our home. I set about cutting down a tree in our backyard and trimming its branches for firewood. Chopping wood is not a particularly strong part of my life, but I went about sawing and chopping like a feeble Paul Bunyan. It wasn't working very well, so I bought a chainsaw. That helped immensely, and soon I had a growing pile of logs in our yard.

This woodpile wasn't neat and tidy; it was a gnarly mess with branches and knots that made splitting the logs into firewood-sized pieces very difficult. I was chopping away with a little hatchet when my neighbor Den, who had every conceivable tool in his workshop, came over with a couple of splitting wedges, two sledgehammers, and a big axe. I was grateful, even though he didn't offer to help me chop up the wood.

I learned that even with the proper tools it is still hard work. Soon I had broken his sledgehammers by cracking the wooden handles, and had even gotten the wedges jammed into logs so deeply that I couldn't get them out no matter how hard I tried. But I was cultivating calluses. Have you noticed how amazing calluses are? First the skin is worn, and starts to break, wear, hurt, and tear—then our bodies, in an incredible display of self-protection, form new layers of skin over the hurting, broken places. With each new layer, the sores heal and the hands become tougher in their sorest spots. It is like God provides our own natural gloves.

I have found the same principle at work in other hurting parts of my life. When relationships create stress points, our emotions are worn down, and our thoughts are bruised from irritation and abuse, we can become callused in our hearts and minds. We can develop tough exteriors to protect us from the hurt and brokenness that await us.

While calluses may be beneficial and even necessary to protect us from the stress and pain of everyday life, they have the side effect of deadening our sensitivity. We feel emotions through a barrier that deadens our experience of life and love. Thus the very thing that protects us from negative input also keeps us from experiencing the positive things that could help us heal.

I noticed a few weeks after my wood-chopping foibles that my new calluses began to peel off and disappear. In their place was fresh, tender new skin. Evidently, underneath the protection of the callus, healing was taking place, and the time came when I didn't need the tough cover of a callus. In fact my hands seem exactly the same as before, except maybe a little softer.

Everyone has hurtful experiences, and calluses form to preserve and protect us during those times. But we need to stay mindful that the tough layers are not meant to be permanent. Underneath the layers healing is taking place, and the time will come when we don't need the calluses anymore. Our brokenness is healed and we are softer because of it.

Albert Einstein observed, "The kind of thinking that will solve the world's problems will be of a different order to the kind of thinking that created those problems in the first place."[1] He was right. More of the same won't fix anything.

When I was on the staff of a large church in Seattle, Washington, I felt way over my head and guilty because of my inadequacies. I wanted to live a better life and be more effective as a person, but I was sure there was something inherently wrong with me. Unlike so many of my friends and colleagues, I was a skeptic. I couldn't help it; I really believed the conspiracy theories, assumed the worst about people, and was outspokenly negative even in the face of great victories and growth in every aspect of our ministry.

Eating lunch one afternoon with my boss, Bruce, I finally confessed my deep distrust and skepticism and pessimism. I asked him to help me. I told him how I needed to learn how to trust people and how to love God more.

For a long time Bruce slowly stirred his cup of soup in silence. I started to feel nervous. Maybe I shouldn't have told my boss the truth about my weaknesses that I had kept hidden for so long. Why would he want someone like the real me on his staff? I stared down in defeat at my salad.

Suddenly, Bruce looked up and asked, "Why do you think you should trust people, John?"

Surprised, I blurted out, "Isn't that the way Christians are supposed to act?" Bruce smiled at me and shared one of the most important truths I've ever learned in my life.

He gently explained how we've gotten it all mixed up. The Bible doesn't command us to trust people, which would be dangerous and foolish. Why would we trust other people when they will inevitably let us down? Then he looked at me for a minute and said, "Besides, you know that you and I can't be trusted either, because we will inevitably let people down, even those who mean the most to us. If we aren't trustworthy in spite of our best efforts, why would we trust others?"

I realized he was right. I had never thought of it that way before. Bruce went on explaining to me that only God is trustworthy. We are to love people and trust God.

Actually trusting God day by day, instead of conjuring up general loving feelings about the Lord of all creation, is a difficult challenge. When we sit around feeling sentimental and "loving" toward God, it doesn't cost us very much. But trusting him to be present in our darkest moments, in our experience of the best and worst of life, is a costly discipleship.

Trusting God in our darkest times will not come easily. What happens to people can be terrible, yet all of us have experienced the unfairness and pain of hurt, betrayal, and loss. But these tragedies are not meant to be the last word. Throughout my life, I've listened to hundreds of people share their experience of healing and grace to overcome the hurts of life. From their stories, I found courage to get past my own brokenness. I learned that the pain we experience today can be transformed by hope and love tomorrow. Life isn't fair, but the sooner we realize this, the sooner we can develop the faith and courage to live in spite of it.

Choosing to love people regardless and choosing to trust God in every situation opens us to come out of our safe, controlled existence and discover the great adventure our life was always meant to be. There are things we'll never get over, it is true. But we can get past them when we take the first steps of choosing to love people and trust God.

12

Walking in the Light while Living in the Shadows

Pain is God's megaphone to rouse a deaf world.

C. S. Lewis

Nothing prepares a parent for the moment they watch attendants take away their child and listen to the doors of the locked psychiatric ward seal shut. I sat in disbelief and wept. A few months earlier our son was senior class president of his high school in Walnut Creek, and now he was entering a mental facility to protect him from suicide.

It has been a journey none of us wanted or anticipated. Watching our son Damian fight for his life in dozens of mental hospitals with countless doctors, medications, therapies, diagnoses, and misdiagnoses has given us empathy for the millions of families that silently wrestle with both the reality and the stigma of mental illness.

There is a shadow world where life is lived apart from the warmth of the sun or the warmth of human love and kindness. People who deal with disabilities in their life have stories of the "other existence," where strangers stare or avoid eye contact but seldom engage as a human being. Loneliness increases, as the person feels like a freak who is being watched but not seen, and judged but not known.

Damian admitted that sometimes he wished he was confined to a wheelchair, "Because then people would know I was disabled and not just dismiss me as weird." Of course everyone's story is different, and their story is their own to tell. So I didn't tell the congregation in Walnut Creek, where I was senior pastor, about the ongoing struggle occurring behind locked doors where my only son was fighting for his life.

For several years I tried to keep our personal world invisible, while my son went through many hospitals, including Stanford Medical Center and Johns Hopkins Psychiatric Center, and through a seemingly endless chain of treatments, including several protocols of electroconvulsive therapy (shock treatments), which reduced him to a drooling vegetable and damaged his short- and long-term memory. During one particularly difficult hospitalization, I finally broke and shared in a sermon about our family's reality. Damian had given permission and told me that he wasn't ashamed, any more than a cancer patient would feel embarrassed or ashamed of their condition.

For the majority of the people in our church it was a significant moment. They responded with compassion and prayerful support. It opened the door for many families to acknowledge that they were going through the same experience, yet like us had never talked about it publicly for fear of people's reactions. But for a small minority of the members, this was unthinkable. The idea of the senior pastor of their prominent church in the middle of their upscale, polished community having this sort of problem was just too much to take. After all, what would the neighbors think? Something had to be done.

The gossip spread like wildfire. Rumors circulated that were bizarre and unreal, yet it seemed the crazier the rumors, the more widespread they became. In time, even Damian began to hear the hurtful and hateful things being said about him throughout the church, and his pain only increased as he blamed himself for problems in the church.

On the positive side, Eileen wanted to find a couple of understanding people who could walk through this nightmare with her. She put a small notice in the church bulletin announcing a support group for moms whose kids were in mental hospitals, jail, or treatment programs. Hoping maybe one or two women might show up, she braced herself for the possibility that she might end up sitting all alone in the room at the church. The meeting night rolled around, and she entered the room to find it full of moms hoping for a chance to share and care. Several mentioned that they never considered even the possibility of talking about their family's greatest struggles at church.

There is no road map for the journey through mental illness. Damian is my hero for continuing to take steps forward even when no hope was in sight. I could never imagine the degree of pain, fear, shame, anxiety, rage, loneliness, and desperation he experienced the past few years. My prayers were reduced to the bare minimum: "Lord, heal my boy." And there were times I probably prayed without much conviction.

When Damian was thirteen years old, he announced that he wanted to be baptized. He was to select a Bible verse to be read at the time of his baptism. He picked one that I didn't like. Why couldn't it be a normal verse like, "Let the children come unto me" or something like that? Not Damian, who resolutely told me that this was his baptism and he'd read the verse he had selected for this moment. Maybe it was a foreshadowing of things to come.

Standing before the congregation, Damian pulled out his Bible and began to read from Psalm 40.

> I waited patiently for the LORD;
> he turned to me and heard my cry.
> He lifted me out of the slimy pit,
> out of the mud and mire;
> he set my feet on a rock
> and gave me a firm place to stand.
> He put a new song in my mouth,
> a hymn of praise to our God.
> Many will see and fear the LORD
> and put their trust in him. (vv. 1–3)

Then his pastor, Bruce Larson, baptized him. Though I fought against Damian's decision at the time, I have returned to those verses time and again, hoping they would be true for our boy.

Heroes in Our Midst

True heroes are all around us, though they might not be noticed as we go on our busy way. I met a man the other day who stopped by to see me with one of our church members.

We enjoyed some amiable conversation, then our discussion suddenly dropped to a different level. He and his wife had been driving up Highway 1 through Maryland when they were hit head-on by a carful of teenagers drag racing over a hill at nearly 100 miles per hour. That split-second impact forever changed their lives. Unlike one of the teens in the other car, they didn't die that night, but the life they knew up until then did.

Five years later, their new lives have been shaped by surgeries, rehab, excruciating and constant pain, post-traumatic flashbacks, anxiety, inability to travel or continue their jobs, and battles with insurance companies that desperately want it to be over, even though it isn't over for them. Yet in the midst of all this, he shared with me the miracle of being spared from bitterness, which would have made their horrible situation even worse. They were able to recognize and celebrate small steps of progress in their recovery, and had a quiet gratefulness in the midst of shattered bones and lives.

Talking on the phone with Georgann, whom I had met through a mutual friend, I was struck by a sense of well-being and calm I didn't expect. Her husband, an executive in the auto industry, had been on his way home from a business trip in Europe. He had been gone for several days and they looked forward to reuniting as a family: dad, mom, and their young son and daughter. That reunion never happened. A terrorist bomb blew up the plane over Lockerbie, Scotland, and life as they knew it was over. Everyone died in the explosion that day.

Over the next couple of decades, she found ways to get past what she would never get over. "I knew that if I let that terrorist act define my life, I would not have a life nor would I be able to help our children," she said. They had to go forward, step by step, building new lives that remembered and honored her husband and her kids' father, but weren't limited by the unthinkable horror of his death.

When I first met Melissa, she was a vivacious, talented young woman working as a graphic designer. It was only later that I realized how heroic she was. In one year her foster brother, her father, and her mother had died. There was no connection between the deaths, each was unique, yet the result was the same. Unspeakable loss and grief hung over Melissa. Longing for a family of her own, she and her husband tried to have children. She miscarried three times. The reality that her life was not ever going to be what she had hoped or imagined weighed upon Melissa heavily. We sat in a Starbucks reflecting on her life while watching her beautiful little adopted daughter play with her coloring books. A new artist was growing up in her family.

Admitting her intolerance for the superficial and often shallow comments she has heard throughout her ordeals, Melissa has a real-life faith tested by the pain of what she'll never get over. Life is not the same, but it is real and it is good.

Dean was a gifted musician. His father had traveled in a band as a harmonica player, and Dean played pedal steel and guitar in several bands in the Bay area. Sundays he'd play in our church with the worship band, and we became friends. One night we went into the city to hear Rock'n'Roll Hall of Famer Richey Furay, formerly of Buffalo Springfield and Poco. I knew that Richey had become a Christian and pastored a church in Colorado, and I was excited to hear him live.

We had a great time at the concert, and Dean got to visit with the pedal steel player in the band. On the way home, he told me he was heading to the beach in Mexico with his wife.

They were bringing his mom and stepdad along for a little vacation in the sun. I wished him well and suggested we get together when he returned from vacation. He never returned.

Dean sent his family home on Saturday and was going to fly back the next day. Somewhere over the ocean near Los Angeles, his plane became the first and only crash in the history of Alaska Airlines. Mechanical failure due to shoddy maintenance caused the plane to suddenly spiral out of the sky, disintegrating into the Pacific Ocean not far from Malibu Beach.

Sitting with his mom and stepdad, we talked about how wrong it feels to outlive our children. "There is a natural order and Dean's death wasn't right," his mom said. They would have gladly changed places with him on that flight. Facing their own deaths would have been much easier than losing their son.

My friend Jim called to share the shocking news that his lively and loving grandson Julian was gone. Grandparents experience a double grief, one for their grandchild and one more for their children, the parents who are devastated by the loss of their child. We cried and shared about the events surrounding the four-year-old's sudden death.

Jim's daughter Emily wrote down her feelings and observations as she went through the unimaginable pain of losing her son. On her blog she wrote,

> My perfect little boy . . . left the planet. No one knows why he got leukemia in the first place, and no one knows why he developed an infection that wasn't even slowed down by the very best doctors using the very best medicine at the very best pediatric hospital in the Midwest. It just happened.

Today, four months after the death of my young son, I don't ask, *Why me?* I don't compare myself to "more fortunate" families who haven't experienced the tragedy of a child's death. It's no coincidence that a book I was reading yesterday included this quote from Helen Keller:

> Instead of comparing our lot with that of those who are more fortunate than we are, we should compare it with the lot of the great majority of our fellow men. It then appears that we are among the privileged.

I have one great big reason to feel less fortunate than others, but I have a whole bunch of reasons to feel privileged. These four months have taught me a lot. Some of it I wish I didn't have to learn. Some of it I appreciate. Today I'm appreciating my new understanding that my pain is not unique. Sooner or later, in big or small ways, we all feel pain. "Why me?" isn't the question to ask. The question to ask is, "Who do we choose to compare ourselves to? What do we choose to feel—unfortunate, or privileged?"[1]

Each of these stories is true, and unique, yet all are connected by the pain in life that forever impacts who we are and who we are becoming. We are choosing to walk in the light, even though our experience is shadowed by the harsh reality of existence.

Sometimes I wonder what life would be like if there were no shadows of pain, distractions, influences, or temptations. It doesn't take long to start blaming the folks around me, thinking if they were better people and were more supportive, I in turn would be a much better person. Of course this line of reasoning is futile, because our lives were never meant to be lived in a hermetically sealed spiritual chamber. More accurate is the idea of our lives being lived in a Petri dish filled with all kinds of strange viruses and bacteria! Jesus said, "In this world you will have trouble, but take heart! I have overcome the world" (John 16:33).

J. B. Phillips wrote, "The real danger . . . lies not in the more glittering and grosser temptations and sins but in a slow deterioration of vision, a slow death of daring courage and willingness to adventure. That's the danger."[2]

At any time, in any circumstance, we have the opportunity to go back to the start and experience the renewal of our minds, emotions, and will through Christ at work in us.

He may be right. Over and over people share about not succumbing to one big temptation or another, and all the while there is a creeping suspicion of a desperate need for renewal of vision, daring, and adventure.

The best definition of renewal that I've heard is, "Renewal is going back to God's original dream for us." What did God have in mind when he first thought of you and me? What is his desire for us today? At any time, in any circumstance, we have the opportunity to go back to the start and experience the renewal of our minds, emotions, and will through Christ at work in us.

In Paul's letter to the church at Philippi, I think we get a glimpse of God's original dream for our lives: "You may become blameless and pure, children of God without fault in a crooked and depraved generation" (Phil. 2:15). Our blameless and pure lives are lived out in the midst of a crooked and depraved world. We are invited by Jesus to walk in the light, but we do it in a very shadowy, sometimes dark, world.

Fault Lines

In every generation there have been some people who advocate dropping out of our crooked culture and pulling away into safe, like-minded communities. But it doesn't work very well. Eating lunch with my friend who is a monk was an interesting experience. Father Francis was Abbot of a Benedictine monastery located in the high desert region above Los Angeles. Since I knew virtually nothing about life in a monastery, I was asking him dumb questions and Francis was showing great patience with his "ignorant friend."

"Isn't life easier," I asked, "when you are removed from the real world and separated from the temptations and influences facing folks down in the city?" He didn't roll his eyes or shake his head in disbelief at my naiveté. He merely gave me a caring smile and responded, "Oh, we didn't leave the world behind when we entered the monastery, we brought it with us." Then he laughed, and said, "Besides, for me to come out and meet you for lunch is not entering the real world. I enter the real world when I return to the monastery."

He had a point. Our lives are meant to be lived in the midst of a mixed-up world. Perhaps that is because then God's power becomes visible to those who have never before experienced his grace, and so we are meant to be right in the thick of things.

But how are we going to be faultless? I'm pretty good at finding fault in people. I'm quick to point out when I think someone is wrong or at fault in any given situation. I am also very quick to point out when I think something is not my fault. Thus blame can be shifted away from me very adeptly. But perhaps there is more to the word *faultless*.

Another use of the word *fault* refers to a fault line, where earthquakes occur. In fact, there is a famous fault line that runs through California called the San Andreas Fault. Its line runs right through the state, and some of the most expensive homes and tallest towers are built on it. In the Bay Area, they even put the pillars holding up the Bay Bridge right on top of the fault line.

Knowing about the fault line didn't keep our family from owning a home subject to frequent earthquakes and tremors. They tended to hit about five o'clock in the morning, while I was lying in bed. Suddenly the whole room would be shaking, lights swinging and knickknacks falling on the floor. After a short time, which feels longer when you are in it, it would be over and I'd roll over and go back to sleep while Eileen would lie there scared to death about what would happen the "next time."

Our tolerance for frightening situations depends on what we are used to, however. Once, when we were in Ireland, Eileen's homeland, we visited some of the towns in Northern Ireland where her family originated. It was during the times of trouble, so we drove through guard stations, and went past heavily armed soldiers in bunkers suitable for a war. In the picturesque town of Inneskillen, where several notorious bombings had occurred, we were eating lunch in a café when our waitress, a pretty young woman, turned and showed us the result of a car bomb—the side of her face and one arm looked melted.

After lunch we drove to a quaint little town of Claugher, where Eileen's relatives had lived. Parking the car in town was difficult because rolls of barbed wire along the sidewalks discouraged street parking near buildings or places that townsfolk might gather. We were in a small shop buying a few items when we struck up a conversation with the teenage girl who worked there.

Finally I got up the courage, or audacity, to ask, "How can you live in a place like this where any minute a bomb might explode, causing untold injury and devastation? This place is too scary for me."

She looked at me for a second, and asked where we were from. "California!" she exclaimed. "I'd never be able to even visit California. They have earthquakes that scare the dickens out of me." Then she spoke of how she feels safer in her hometown than she would ever feel in shaky old California. Isn't it weird how we can get used to our earthquakes to the extent they no longer bother us, but are frightened of what might happen somewhere unfamiliar?

I can picture that, like physical fault lines below the surface of the earth, we have fault lines deep inside our hearts and minds. In times of extreme pressure our internal plates shift and we have inner turmoil of clashing values, emotions, and thoughts. At first we remain smooth on the surface, but soon we erupt with earthquake-like force. It can be scary to watch and even more frightening to experience.

When the Bible admonishes us to be "without fault" in this crooked generation, it is a call to reconnect the clashing that occurs below the surface. We can have integrity within that matches what is occurring on the surface, and be basically the same on the inside as we are on the outside. *Authentic* is a word we use to describe such people—those who don't appear as one thing but are really something else.

Our world is longing to see people who demonstrate true authenticity. Tired of pretense and posturing, we are open to anyone who demonstrates a genuine transparency in the midst of all we experience in this world. I believe that is part of God's dream for us: living in the real world with authenticity, vulnerability, and transparency.

I believe that is part of God's dream for us: living in the real world with authenticity, vulnerability, and transparency.

When we have an experience that we'll never get over, it changes us. The nagging pain stays with us below the surface. We can feel as if we're wandering through our days in an in-between world. We aren't necessarily sick, but we don't feel well either.

It can be difficult even for our friends to know how to relate to us. We can appear zoned out, neither connecting well nor bringing our usual level of positive energy to the relationship.

Following a painful experience in my life when I felt betrayed and rejected, I remember walking through a supermarket feeling more like a ghost than a man. I may have appeared normal to the other shoppers passing by, but inside I felt different, distant, and awkward. I hoped I could get my shopping done without running into anyone I knew. No such luck. Coming around the corner of an aisle was an energetic young lady from the church where I had recently been pastor.

There were lots of smiles and good wishes exchanged. I even managed to coax some positive expressions into my speech and flourished a bit of a frozen smile. As I made my escape past the bottles of pasta sauce, I felt dead inside. What had become of me? Would I ever feel "solid" again? I started to cry. Rather than feeling better, I went on in the in-between world pretending I was fine, even though I wasn't.

Looking below the Surface

Many people who live with constant pain report that there comes a time when it moves from the low-level range right into the piercing jab of hurt that lets you know something is terribly wrong. Each person experiences this in a slightly different way. For me it was the lightning flash of realizing my life was shattered into a mountain of little shards and pieces that would never be put back together again. My life was broken. It hurt.

This level of pain changed how I perceived the world around me. Suddenly the world seemed sinister, people seemed evil, and noticing strangers quietly discussing something made me suspicious, even paranoid that I was left out and would never again be included.

My suspicious and distrusting perspectives led me to hold people at a distance to keep from being hurt by them. Positive comments to me were dismissed and discarded in the light of the betrayal I had experienced. Negative comments that I might have overlooked in the past now grew in intensity and chewed on my heart. It almost seemed that I was collecting evidence to prove I really was the loser my betrayers portrayed me to be.

It became easy for me to make snap judgments about total strangers without bothering to get to know them. I thought people wouldn't want to know me, so maybe I could dismiss people instantly by stereotyping them and not taking them seriously . . . until it happened to me.

I was down on Aurora Boulevard in Seattle, getting a radio put in our car. Aurora is a stretch of strip malls that runs from the Seatac airport in the south all the way to Everett in

190

the north. It could be described as a "working area," since some of the men are working and there are lots of "working women" on the street.

I had a few hours to kill while waiting for my car, so I walked down to a St. Vincent de Paul thrift store where I bought several low-cost treasures and trinkets. I even got a first-edition copy of *Black Beauty* for five dollars. Carrying my loot in several St. Vincent de Paul bags, I made my way up Aurora and stopped for lunch at Sunny's Teriyaki.

As I set my bags on a table, I heard the owner yell at me, "No use bathroom, unless you buy something!" I assured him that I was there to eat lunch and I had the money to pay for it, no problem.

As I began to eat my spicy chicken and rice with a nice side salad, the owner came out to see me and placed a long, thin blue card on the table in front of my plate. Glancing at my thrift store bags, he said confidently, "This will help you with your problems!" I glanced at the card and it had a list of about a dozen Alcoholics Anonymous groups that were meeting in the area.

Assuming it was just a good-natured misunderstanding, I thanked him for his thoughtfulness and continued eating my way-too-spicy chicken. By now I'm pretty sure my face was turning red and I was sweating through my shirt from the hot peppers. About ten minutes later he returned to my table. "You have girlfriend or wife?" he asked.

I assured him that I had been married to Eileen for several decades. Without pausing to listen, he quickly pointed to the bottom part of the blue card and said, "This will help her with her problems!" Glancing down to where he pointed, I saw the Narcotics Anonymous groups and their meeting times.

Smiling, I thanked him, then just to clarify I pointed out that despite my thrift store bags and the fact that I was walking along the street, I wasn't an alcoholic and Eileen was definitely not a drug addict, though I did appreciate his attempts to be of help. He just rolled his eyes and said, "Yeah, sure but this could really help you with your problems," as he walked back into the kitchen.

Now that I have been profiled and stereotyped and written off as a hopeless indigent, I regret that Sunny missed a chance to get to know me. Who knows—he might have been able to help me with one of my many real problems!

Pain hurts. Why are we surprised? Sure, we expect to hurt if we fall and break our arm. Why, then, are we surprised when we fall and break our heart? One small difference between a broken bone and a broken heart is that we assume the bone will mend, but we suspect the heart will never be set right.

This can lead us to the horrible realization that if we ever let people close enough to know us like our betrayers knew us, they might recognize the same inadequacies in us and hurt us all over again.

Lloyd John Ogilvie, retired chaplain of the US Senate, has said that for us to be vulnerable means we give someone else the weapons that can hurt us. When I first heard him say this, it rang true. It also explained why I found it so difficult to be vulnerable even with those closest to me.

I was pretty adept at giving others weapons that could never really hurt me. Issues and problems that happened in the past, which I had already worked through and resolved, could be shared. But I didn't want anyone knowing what I currently struggled with.

Slowly I began to make intentional choices to share more vulnerably when the opportunity arose. In time my confidence grew and I found myself sharing more easily until I was actually handing out loaded weapons of the emotional kind to anyone who asked.

It was only a matter of time until some of those lethal weapons, in the hands of the wrong people, turned back in my direction. I was shot down by the people with whom I had been the most vulnerable. When it happened, I was unprepared for the ferocity of the attack launched against me. Ironically, most of the accusations were simply things I had shared in a moment of vulnerability, but in the hands of unloving people they took on a powerful destructive force.

Would I ever be vulnerable again? The temptation was strong to put up a false front, give measured responses, and present a robust persona to the world. Over lunch I complained to a friend about my desire to stop sharing with other people. I complained that since others didn't share vulnerably, I didn't want to either. "Besides," I said, "often when I do share, and it gets used against me, it hurts." My friend sat for a moment, chewing his sandwich. "Why would you let what unhealthy people do or don't do make you stop being healthy? Why give them the power to determine what kind of person you are going to be?" he asked. Then he smiled and said, "Besides, can't you be authentic and vulnerable just because it makes you healthy? Forget about what the sick people think."

I realize now how wise my friend was. We don't need to take our signals about our health and lifestyle from those around us. We don't need to allow the choices of others to determine how we will live and respond to the challenges of life. The kind of courage needed to walk in the light while living in the shadows doesn't happen easily or quickly. It can be frustrating to those of us who are tired of working at getting past what we'll never get over. Perhaps we can learn to celebrate our unfinishedness.

Bruce Larson frequently reminded people that they were unique, unrepeatable miracles, a gift from God. He even said it about me. But I wasn't ready to believe him. Maybe I thought that if I could just get over some things, then I'd be able to accept it. Of course, as you already know, we aren't ever going to get over it. Not this side of heaven. But as I take steps to get past my brokenness, I'm surprised to discover my friend Bruce was right. I'm unique. There is only one of me, and no one else in the whole world will ever have the experiences, successes, failures, struggles, joys, and relationships that I have had in my life. This is also true of you. All of us, regardless of struggles and setbacks, are unrepeatable miracles. But how are we a gift from God?

I had trouble seeing myself as God's gift to anyone. Then I began to see how powerful it was when someone else made the effort to honestly share their life with me. Our lives were never meant to be lived solely for ourselves. Life takes on new meaning and purpose when it is shared. Your story, with all its humanity and authenticity, is a gift that can bring encouragement, meaning, and even hope to those with whom you share it. There is power in sharing even our unfinished experience. Don't wait until there is a complete and totally victorious ending to your story. That may never come.

We also honor people by taking the time to listen to their unique story. It is a rare gift to ask someone to share their experience of brokenness, loss, and healing. I'm discovering that the more I hear people relate their sagas of getting past what they will never get over, the more I appreciate and value their presence in my life. Take the time to listen and connect—it will enrich your life and bless someone else.

13

Glancing Back
while Moving Forward

Life is a great adventure or it is nothing.

Helen Keller

The beginning is never the beginning. In order to move forward, there must first be an ending. Otherwise we merely accumulate emotional baggage and carry our burdens from one situation to another. Perhaps a lot of our struggle to get past what we'll never get over is that we try to get a fresh start before we put an end to the past.

Tim Hansel was an author and speaker who shared from his experience about living his life in spite of constant pain. Having broken his back in a mountain climbing fall, his reflections in the book *You Gotta Keep Dancing* were authentic and insightful. When my son was entering high school, we heard Tim at what would turn out to be one of his last speaking engagements. After the talk (which went on for a couple of hours), Damian announced that Tim was "the greatest speaker I have ever heard!" Visiting with Tim afterwards, he told him about some of the struggles he was facing, and Tim gave him a small memento: a lapel button with three words. "Stop—Change—Start."

Damian still has that button. Through his turbulent growing up years, struggle with mental illness, and fight against the lure of suicide, he kept the reminder from Tim that in order to grow there were steps to take. I'm going to borrow those three words from Tim's button.

Stop

Perhaps our attempts to change have been frustrating or ineffective simply because we skip the step of ending our present situation, avoid the uncomfortable time of transition and turbulence associated with change, and jump right over to attractive "new beginnings."

Endings are fearful. They break our connection with ourselves and they awaken old feelings of hurt and shame. When I was facing a job transition, I didn't want to be adrift while seeking new employment. To avoid that uncomfortable time of adjustment, I lined up a new opportunity, scheduled our move to a new city where my wife and I put in an offer on a new home, and pictured ourselves safely adapting to the new environment. Only then did I resign my current job, list our house for sale, and share the news with our friends and family. It all happened fast, and our life was buzzing with activities that kept us occupied and too tired to consider options or outcomes. Looking back, now I can see that I am not at all comfortable with the frightening "in-between" stage where healthy change occurs.

I like the idea of change; it is the changing I struggle with. Even though in my lifetime there has been an amazing amount of change, and everywhere I look I am reminded that there is more change ahead, I still resist changing even when I know it will be for the better.

Personally, I find it almost pathologically impossible to let go (even though I wrote a book with Dr. Bobbie Reed, *Building Strong People*, that was all about letting go of control in order to empower leaders[1]). I have trouble letting go of the past, of old hurts, and even of my "old school" ways. Maybe that is why I have so much clutter in my room as well as in my mind.

I don't think there's much chance that anyone will accuse me of being a clean freak. I seem to have no genetic disposition to throw anything away. Life would be much simpler if I could just toss some stuff now and then. Maybe a total snow-plowing of the garage isn't required, but perhaps a thorough paring down would be beneficial. I'm not a crazy hoarder; I just keep things long after they have any useful purpose, perhaps in an effort to hold on to pieces of my life.

The problem is the quantity and variety of these treasured keepsakes. I have a closet full of old suits and sport coats, many with strange lapels or design features that guarantee they will never come back in style. Then there are the boxes of stamp collections going back to childhood, even though I never get them out and look at them, much less work on the collection. In our last move, I hauled over one hundred and twenty very heavy boxes of books cross-country in a moving truck, simply because I didn't want to let them go.

Of course it doesn't stop there. I also have old record albums, rusted tools, even a collection of china dish sets that could serve an army (should the army need to eat off antique bone china from England).

For me it's not just about collecting things, it's more about not being able to let anything go. The real difficulty for me is that what I do with stuff around the house I also do with memories and emotional baggage: I carry them around, telling myself that they might be useful someday. Of course, someday never comes.

In the book *Letting Go*, the authors warn against looking back on our loss too soon or in unhealthy ways. They compare getting out pictures, mementos, or other things that remind us of our loss to repeatedly checking a toothache. The temptation to pull out a special reminder is like

> poking your tongue into a cavity or sucking cold air onto it or biting down on a new filling to see if it is still tender. . . . Don't indulge a masochistic urge to look at an object connected to the old relationship, just to see if it still has the power to make you feel sad. It probably does.[2]

I'm certainly not recommending that kind of counterproductive emotional flagellation. I do not suggest glancing back with a longing gaze, or indulging in a regretful reminiscence. Instead, we are able to glimpse the bigger picture briefly and affirm ourselves for the progress we have made. Perspective comes when we acknowledge steps we have taken to change and grow for the future.

By jumping ahead to a new beginning before we address the need to end our current situation, we bypass the change experience and all the uncertainty that goes with it. Unfortunately, it eventually catches up with us, and then we are faced with untangling a mess from our avoided transitions.

Change

It can be very unsettling to undergo change, even in the best of times. When we are getting past what we'll never get over, change can feel confusing and even frightening. This is certainly not a new phenomenon. When Alice went down the rabbit hole, her world was turned upside down.

> "Who are you?" said the Caterpillar. . . .
>
> "I—I hardly know, sir, just at present," Alice replied rather shyly, "At least I know who I was when I got up this morning. But I think I must have been changed several times since then."[3]

One of my friends told me about a new word she had learned, *liminality*, which refers to waiting on the threshold. She explained it is the place where the passage behind us has closed, yet the options before us have yet to be revealed. It involves moving from one identity to another or one place to another, but we remain in that "in-between" state. Most of us try to rush into something, anything, rather than waiting for the future to be revealed. It isn't a pleasant place to be, but that's when we grow most.

Jesus said, "Unless a kernel of wheat falls to the ground and dies, it remains only a single seed. But if it dies, it produces many seeds" (John 12:24). He then went on to apply this truth to humanity, pointing out that if we try to hold on to our life as it is, we will lose it, but if we let go we can find life in its fullest.

Too often I've struggled to keep old dreams alive, old connections vital, and old memories vivid. When we let go of our need to control the world and the people in it, we begin an adventure that leads to a full and purposeful life.

When we let go of our need to control the world and the people in it, we begin an adventure that leads to a full and purposeful life.

Change is hard. Talking about change is easy—until we actually do it. What makes change difficult is the inherent experience of disorientation and disengagement. These experiences can be challenging, because letting go of our identity and connections that have helped us define who we are is painful.

When we go through a painful loss such as getting fired from our job or having our spouse announce they are divorcing us, our whole way of ordering our world and determining our place in the universe is flipped upside down. Who are we if we aren't defined by our career or our marriage? Who knows?

Sometimes instead of addressing our disorientation, we'll quickly jump to a new job or into a new relationship, thus postponing the inevitable. Of course, when we skip the in-between phase, we don't get a new beginning. Rather we often carry much of our old baggage, attitudes, and problems with us and dump them into our new situation. No wonder we soon find the same difficulties, conflicts, and struggles emerging in our "new" situation.

Jesus's comparison of life to the death and rebirth process of wheat doesn't make our transition experience any easier—or less painful. We just have a bigger perspective from which to view the changes we are experiencing. For the vast majority of people without this perspective who face the upheaval of their reality, "they are caught between positive thinking and despair, keeping themselves going by lighting matches and whistling in the dark."[4]

Going through the experience of being "in-between" in the very core of change can be both frightening and discouraging. It is a time when we are most vulnerable, because we are emotionally adrift and not sure what will happen to us and to those we love. Leo Tolstoy wrote about his own experience in transition:

> I felt that something had broken within me on which my life had always rested, that I had nothing left to hold on to, and that morally my life had stopped. And yet I could give no reasonable meaning to any actions of my life. And I was surprised that I had not understood this from the very beginning. My state of mind was as if some wicked and stupid jest was being played upon me by someone. . . . [I asked myself] what will be the outcome of what I do today or what I shall do tomorrow? What will be the outcome of all my life? Why should I live? Why should I do anything?[5]

We want our effort to matter, and I believe we all want to grow. It is necessary for sustaining life and becoming the men and women we know we can be. The problem is that growth cannot occur without change. Unless we make clear choices to effect tangible changes in our behaviors, thinking, strategies, and relationships, growth is not a possibility for us.

Growth, Change, and Conflict

Organizations can also set growth goals and even bring in new leadership to implement the changes needed to reach those goals. However, when the changes begin to occur, conflicts arise between the old guard and the new leaders. Because conflict is usually uncomfortable, it is determined that for the sake of peace, the new leaders will be let go, the changes will cease, and the old order will be reaffirmed. This often results in a season of decline, until new growth goals are affirmed and the process repeats itself.

What is true for organizations, businesses, and churches is also true for individuals. Though the desire to grow remains strong, it is often blocked because growth comes only through change. We live in a fast-changing world, and it takes effort to adapt to the changes all around us. Growth cannot happen without change, and change cannot occur without conflict.

When we begin to undertake the steps necessary for our personal growth, we begin to implement changes in our actions, attitudes, and approaches to life. These changes create tension, resulting in conflict. Sometimes it is inner conflict, such as new behaviors combating old attitudes or beliefs. Other times it is interpersonal conflict, such as the stress that inevitably surfaces when a person with an addiction enters a recovery program, and the members of their family struggle to adjust to the "new" person in their midst.

Anyone who seeks to grow must choose to go through the conflicts that will inevitably surface. Maintaining the status quo isn't healthy, but it can be peaceful. If we totally stop growing there will be no more conflicts and everything will be peaceful. Just visit a cemetery, and notice what a peaceful, conflict-free environment it is. No growth results in death. Life moves forward, taking risks and experiencing a great adventure along the way.

Our inability to change may be the one thing that keeps us from getting past what we'll never get over. Studies have shown that even when faced with the possibility of dying without change, most people still won't do it.

Start

This final step in Tim Hansel's lapel button can be invigorating. A fresh start with a new beginning helps us see opportunities that may have been previously overlooked. A friend used to tell me how much he liked "first annuals." He became invigorated whenever he was involved in a new endeavor, but he hated the "second annual." He explained that when a new project is successful, the next time around people expect the same enthusiasm and uplift they experienced the first time. But inevitably, there is a letdown and disappointment creeps in.

It is an encouraging sign when we begin to emerge from the painful experiences of life. Cautiously at first, then with increasing boldness, we step out and become involved in life with courage and wisdom.

For the Adventurous Spirit

When we moved back to Seattle and accepted the challenge to plant a new church in a region purported to have the lowest church attendance in the country, I didn't even know where to begin. I had no experience in starting something from scratch, but I was sure it had to be unique and different, because I needed a change. One of my first encounters was having breakfast with a person who had started several successful businesses. I hoped he would give me some ideas for our new opportunity.

"Who are you trying to reach with this new Harbor Church?" he asked as soon as we got our food. Sitting across from him at the 5-Spot cafe on Queen Anne Hill, I was eating the "special" breakfast, which had a weird blend of eggs, peppers, and pulled pork (carnitas). "Are you going to target a particular age group, or life stage, or what?" Then he asked what kind of people I wanted to hang out with.

If we knew all the answers and had everything figured out, life wouldn't be an adventure— it would just be a commute!

I started to squirm a little inside, not wanting to limit who God might bring into our fellowship. At the same time, I didn't want to sound like I had no plan or focus. So I answered, "I want a church for the adventurous spirit." Then I thought that could be the mission for our new church.

I want to go somewhere with a group of fellow travelers who have an adventurous spirit. That is what Jesus calls us to do. "Come, follow me," he invites. Like the first disciples, we wonder what is in store, what we will experience along the way, who we will meet that will shape our lives in meaningful ways, and what obstacles we will confront that require us to help each other as we overcome.

If we knew all the answers and had everything figured out, life wouldn't be an adventure—it would just be a commute! Why do so many of us go through life feeling like commuters stuck in traffic? It seems as if everyone is sitting in their own private vehicles, tuned out to what is going on in the lives of those around them as they creep down the spiritual highway in slow motion, frustrated and sometimes stewing about the inconvenience of having so many people ahead of them. Sometimes they think that life would be better if those others weren't there, but the monotony sets in and they end up just fitting in, going through the motions, hoping nothing bad happens. What a drag. No wonder most people can't stand their dull routine; it is no different than our boring efforts to get to work.

In Seattle there is a famous sculpture of commuters waiting for a ride. It is called, "Waiting for the Interurban." Because it looks lifelike, many drivers go right past it without noticing; it looks like an average bus stop in a busy city. It consists of life-size statues of people waiting endlessly for the ride that never comes. There is even a dog standing in the group. Evidently the mayor of Seattle at the time fought to stop funding for the arts in the city. So the artist put the mayor's face on the dog as a whimsical insult to his opponent. The mayor probably didn't think it was funny, but the statue stands, reminding us of the drudgery of daily routine.

We all need an adventure. I want to feel the adrenaline kick in when I hear people share about their real lives and real faith. I want to know the joy that comes from sharing deeply and caring deeply. I want to feel the tension of going beyond my comfort zone to take some risks in life, beyond the security of my own control. I want a life for the adventurous spirit!

Friedrich Nietzsche observed, "Believe me, the secret for harvesting from existence the greatest fruitfulness and the greatest enjoyment is to live dangerously!"[6] Taking steps forward toward health and hope is a risk worth taking. A friend once advised me, "If you have a choice between doing something safe and something risky, always take the risk." We can live lives of adventure and meaning, encouraging others to come with us on the journey.

In the early stages of getting past what we'll never get over, the very idea of risk-taking or adventure might seem incomprehensible. To a certain extent that is understandable, because when we experience loss, we don't think we could survive another letdown. Our need for self-protection is quite strong and we often don't think we even have the strength to venture out of our home. That is to be expected. However, when we alter our perception of adventure and risk to fit our unique stage of recovery, we can see that even small steps forward can feel like a huge risk to us at the time.

At every step along the way, consider your options and see if one is more risky than the other. Without being foolhardy, choose to step a little beyond your comfort zone. You might be surprised at how strong and energized you become.

When we try to control things, they have to get smaller. In the same way, when I try to control my life or the people and things I'm involved in, my world grows smaller, my friends pull away, and my projects fail to thrive. But when I begin to let go, little by little, my circle of friends expands, work opportunities increase, and I begin to develop a zest for life.

From time to time, it is helpful to glance back as we move forward. Not the longing gaze of regret or wishful thinking, and certainly not the glare of bitterness and unforgiveness; rather, these are glances that illumine how far we have come. They allow us to appreciate our life and experiences from a new perspective. Rather than pulling us down, they can invigorate us for the new experiences awaiting us. We learn from each mistake and misplaced trust along the way, and make better choices because of the pain we have endured.

In my mind, the houses we lived in during my childhood were large, expansive, and filled with details that contribute to my memories. When I revisited the house my father built in Whittier, California, I was stunned to find it had shrunken in size and scope. The huge yards where we played were mere patches of grass and dirt. The large rooms were in fact tiny, and it seemed amazing that our family was able to fit into such a small house.

Likewise, as we get past our pain we can glance back and see people, problems, and situations from our new reality. Those things shrink down in the context of our new reality, and they lose their power to define and control us.

A few years ago, we were in New York City and wanted to visit the site of the 9/11 tragedy. I reserved a room in the Hilton just across the street. We were given a room with a panoramic view of the site. In the early morning hours, just before sunrise, Eileen woke up and looked out the window. She woke me up to say that something was happening on the street below our window. Sleepily, I found my glasses and looked down to see a long row of police cars pulling up to the 9/11 site with their emergency lights flashing.

At first I thought another terrorist act had brought so many police officers to the scene. Then we watched as the police officers got out of their cars and lined up at the spot where so many friends, fellow officers, and everyday people had been injured or killed on that day we remember so well. After a moment of silence, they returned to their vehicles and quietly drove up the street to begin their workday policing and protecting the city.

Later that morning, I asked the hotel doorman about the strange scene we had witnessed. I asked if anything like this had happened before, or if it was a special event of some kind. He explained that the officers gathered at the site each morning as they began or ended their shifts. "It helps them remember why they do what they do, and how important it is for all of us."

I've thought about that eerie scene we silently witnessed from our hotel window. This quiet act of honoring fallen comrades inspires them to get past what they will never get over. And we too are survivors. Our life today is valuable. Perhaps it's time to see ourselves as a unique, unrepeatable miracle, the gift that God always intended us to be.

Steps for the Journey

The ABCs of Self-Care

Thank you for walking with me through this book and allowing me to share some of the experiences that can help us discover new possibilities for living each day. I invite you to explore some practical steps that can lead to a more nurturing, adventurous life. I offer this "Alphabet of Steps" as a few tangible ways to help you get past what you'll never get over. Regardless of the issues or struggles we face, there are options to consider and actions to take that can be uplifting and life-affirming.

A Ask yourself the hard questions, such as, "What is the worst thing that can happen?" Once we know the worst, it is easier to consider the options objectively without the distraction of free-floating anxiety. Facing potential setbacks with an idea of how bad it might get helps us determine the limits of our loss or pain. There can even be a sense of freedom when we've considered the cost and realize that we will still survive.

B Begin again. A fresh start can invigorate us emotionally, physically, relationally, and spiritually. Sometimes we feel frustrated that nothing works or we can't make anything turn out right. By stepping back and experiencing a new beginning, we open ourselves to the invigoration and excitement that come with starting an adventure. Ask yourself: If you could go back to the beginning and start anew, what would you do differently?

C Make a **change** of your own choosing. We can feel overwhelmed by the changes being forced on us by others; we also can assume we have no viable choices. But when we choose to try something new and different, it can be empowering. It is easy to feel stuck in old patterns that leave us feeling powerless to make a difference. Making even a small change gives us encouragement that we are not prisoners of our past, but have the ability to make choices that in time lead to health and hope.

D **Discover** the world around you. Take observant walks and intentionally notice little things that might be overlooked when driving in a car. Even walking a few blocks makes a difference. It helps burn stress, increases oxygen in our bodies, and interrupts the monotonous routine of sedentary life. Discover opportunities to have an adventure. This doesn't have to be expensive or exotic; you can visit a museum in town, take a day trip to a nearby city, or tour a factory. It is amazing

how many things are waiting for us to discover them. I lived in the Bay Area for thirteen years and never got around to visiting Alcatraz. Tourists flock there from all over the world, but I lived a few miles away and never saw it.

E **Express** appreciation and affirmation. Write a note, or send a card for no special occasion other than letting someone know you appreciate them. Take a moment to notice the name of the checker at the grocery store or the busboy in the café. Call them by name and thank them for assisting you. When you see a military person in uniform, thank them for their service. Be on the lookout for opportunities to affirm people around you. Once, when we were getting off a plane, I turned to a young mom with two small children and said, "They are such great travelers, you must be a wonderful mother." The kids looked up at amazement, and she lit up with a smile. She whispered that she'd worried the whole flight that the kids might disturb other travelers. They walked off the plane with joy and relief.

F **Forgive** someone even if they may not deserve it. Don't tell them, just do it. Maintain a healthy perspective. Remember there is forgiveness for you and others. Apologize to those you have hurt or wronged. It will help you feel free, and release you from the guilt you deservedly feel. Perhaps the person you need to forgive first is yourself. Go ahead and do it. Asking forgiveness, and also making amends if possible, can open the door for you to forgive yourself as well as others.

G Cultivate a **garden**. A few herbs, tomatoes, or flowers can make a difference. In a time when there is not much closure, it helps to watch something grow that we have planted with our own hands. It doesn't have to be large. A simple planter or box on a deck is a good place to begin. Who knows, we might get lucky and actually be able to eat fresh from the garden.

H **Help** someone in such a way that they don't know who to thank. Tune in to another's needs, then help them anonymously. A bag of groceries on the porch or a gift card in the mailbox is a great surprise for needy families in the neighborhood. Order a large pizza to be delivered to a single-parent family. Believe me, they will remember and be amazed that someone cared enough to think of them. Besides, if they don't know who was kind to them, they'll have to be nice to everyone

. . . who knows, anyone could be the helping stranger.

I **Invest** in the people around you. Begin to notice and acknowledge the gardener in the park, the bus driver, the waitress, the cashier at McDonald's, or even the greeter at Target. Call them by name, introduce yourself, and treat them like the valuable person they are. It will bless you and them. My wife began what she called her "restaurant ministry." Every day she'd eat lunch by herself (with a book) in the same restaurant, and make an effort to get to know the staff. Soon they all knew her and came by to talk with her, and she prayed for them and treated them like valued friends. In time, that is what they become. She still gets cards and letters from waitresses in cities where we used to live. They continue to stay in touch and care for each other. (Of course, be sure to tip generously!)

J **Join** a small group. We can be lonely in a crowd, but a regular time with a few people allows us to know and be known, which can be a pretty good foundation for allowing ourselves to be loved. No complicated program or study guide is needed. Just give yourself an opportunity to check in and share some of your story. You might choose to read and discuss a book together, or a passage of Scripture, and commit to pray for each other during the week. In groups I've been in, the leadership was assigned to whoever brought the donuts that week. Thus everyone had their turn at being the "leader."

K Kindle the flame within you. It is not uncommon, when we go through difficult situations, to feel deadness inside. Perhaps our dreams have been squelched or our esteem has been crushed and we no longer feel passionate about anything. I encourage you to nurture and value your passion. Allow yourself to come alive and begin to care, feel, and express yourself with freedom and even intensity. There are always those who would throw water on our dreams and remind us why something may not be reasonable. But kindle the tiny sparks of creativity, intuition, artistic expression, and kindness anyway. In time they might burst into a flame of energy that may surprise you.

L Become a lifetime learner. Enroll in a class, since there is no time like a bad time to step out and learn on our own terms. Once when I was going through a difficult job transition I decided not to waste the painful experience, so I went to a

local community college and began to learn Spanish. It helped me get through the painful season of loss because I had a goal and something positive to work toward. There are plenty of things to learn. You could take a writing class or learn to paint. I recently took a watercolor class, and though I have no talent, it was fun and I enjoyed meeting new people. (I even have a half-finished painting to show for my efforts.) You could learn to cook: serve friends a special meal. Use the food channels on cable television or local cooking classes to experiment with preparing foods you might never have tried before. Pick an ethnic food or regional specialties like Cajun, Thai, or southwestern. Other regions often have favorite foods that might seem strange to us until we try them. (And some seem strange even after we try them—but the trial is worthwhile.)

M Add music to your life. Join the choir at church or a community singing group. Take lessons to play a musical instrument or practice one you haven't played in years. If nothing else, listen to music. It is a needed tonic. Music touches us on an emotional level and can inspire us for action or soothe us when we get ruffled. I just bought a banjo. I know it sounds weird, but have you ever considered how hard it is to play sad, gloomy songs on a banjo?

N Explore social **networks** like Facebook or LinkedIn to find and reconnect with old friends from various eras in your life. I've been amazed when folks I used to know surface and we begin to communicate and reconnect in various ways. These networks remind us what a gift friendship can be, and help facilitate easy communication. If you are looking for a place to start, you are welcome to begin with me. I invite you to be my Facebook friend, or check out my website: www.jwestfall.com.

O **Organize** your environment. Structure reduces anxiety. When we feel bad, it is easy to let things go (and grow) until we are buried in clutter and disorder. Start with something tangible, like choosing to simplify your closet. Weed through your clothes and donate the extras to a local thrift store. It is amazing how much we've hung on to that can be released. Personally, this can be hard for me to do. I often go through my stuff and then put it all back without letting anything go. Sometimes I have to set a goal, such as filling two bags of clothes to donate, so that I actually do what I say I want to do.

P **Practice** thankfulness. Start the day by making a list of five things for which you are thankful. This year I was determined to be intentionally thankful. Since I had the habit of quickly shifting into negative thoughts, I forced myself to seek out things I could be thankful about. I have now made a commitment to write and send a thank-you note each day for a year. If I miss a day, then I have to make it up by doing two the next day. It doesn't come easy or naturally for me yet, but I hope in time this new habit will be part of how I live my life: with gratitude.

Q **Quit** something. Address your addictions. Addictive behavior can take many forms: drinking, drugs, eating, gambling, smoking, shopping, and sex, to name a few. If we can acknowledge them, we can seek available help and move forward. Be careful that you don't get hooked on "sympathy addiction." It isn't necessary to continually tell everyone what happened to you. Sharing with a friend you trust can help you clarify your thoughts and help you sort out the feelings instead of just reliving them. This is a good time to resist the urge to self-pity or self-medicate, to admit we are powerless, and to begin the steps to recovery.

R Ride a train. Visit a place you have never been, or get somewhere familiar in a new way. I recently went on a train expedition with Eileen. We took the train from Seattle to Portland, explored the city, stayed overnight, and caught the return train the next day. It was completely different from our usual habit of driving around and not really experiencing much beyond the inside of our car.

S Surprise someone in a whimsical way. Regardless of our circumstances, we have the power to bring unexpected joy into another person's life. Send flowers or a card to encourage and uplift someone in your life. Years ago when we were struggling grad students with no money, someone put cash in an envelope and left it in our mailbox with an anonymous note encouraging us to use the cash for a date night, not for bill paying. It wasn't a lot of money, but the gesture was huge to us.

T Test reality. Not all assumptions are true; neither are all of our fears. In the same way that electric wiring needs to be grounded, our perceptions and emotional responses also need to be grounded—in reality. Check out their accuracy,

ask good questions, and get feedback from people you trust. You can also do a self-assessment. Make a list of your strengths and weaknesses, including those things that make you a unique individual. Try to nurture your strengths instead of merely repairing your weaknesses.

U Allow your **uniqueness** to shine. Don't forget that you are a unique individual, a miraculous gift from God. There is no one else in the entire world just like you. Your style, perspectives, appearance, and inner thoughts are yours alone. If we were all the same, imagine how boring our world would be. Make a list of the qualities and characteristics that show your uniqueness. Even things that may seem to be disabilities or weaknesses can be recognized as aspects of our uniqueness that contribute to making us the person we are. Resist the temptation to "fit in" or "go along." The world doesn't need any more people who are just alike, but it does need the one and only you!

V Volunteer in the church and the community. Get out, get involved, get going, and give back. Sign up to help at special events like golf tournaments, county fairs, art galleries, museums, charity auctions, and fund-raising banquets; care for kids in Sunday school or youth group; usher at a regional theater for plays and concerts; or volunteer at the YMCA or Boys and Girls Clubs. Most events need volunteers to help in various ways. It can easily turn into a fun experience for you. At our church we volunteer to serve food at the Seahawks football games in partnership with a local restaurant chain. We get out and serve burgers and garlic fries to the fans, and the restaurant makes a charitable donation to our ministry. Everyone benefits.

W Write a letter—not an email or a postcard. I'm always pleasantly surprised when I receive a real letter. It sends the message that the writer took time to think about me and my situation, to share their thoughts, and to actually address an envelope, put a stamp on it, and take it out to the mailbox. Maybe it's old school, but a letter is a great gift. Why not write a letter to God? Sometimes when I find it hard to pray, I get out a piece of paper and write to God. I'll start out, "Dear God," then proceed to write about my day. Then I write about what I'm feeling at the time, ask a question or two, and wrap up with an expression of appreciation. During

the most difficult times in my life, this helped me connect with God in a tangible way while clarifying what I was experiencing at the time.

We can also start writing in a journal. Begin to write daily entries including what is happening and how you are feeling. Describe issues and conflicts, ask questions, and include prayer requests for you and others. Looking back, you will be astounded at the tangible record of your growth and life. Writing about your feelings and frustrations as well as hopes and dreams can help you understand how things may have happened, and how you might make different choices in the future.

X The **X factor.** Your life matters to God. I believe we were never meant to get through this world without some bruises and scars. I have found that I need to invite Jesus Christ to come into all the areas of my life and help me get past what I'll never get over. Believe me, it is too difficult to go through stuff alone. Jesus promises to never leave us or forsake us, and there have been times when I know I couldn't have gone on without his presence, power, and love to get me through. Say yes to Christ and let him walk with you on the journey.

Y Take care of YOU. Give yourself time to heal. It is easy to subtly pressure ourselves to "hurry up and get better." Allowing time for healing and new beginnings is a marvelous gift we can give ourselves. Treat yourself to a massage. Our bodies carry tension that limits our flexibility and results in nagging aches and pains. A therapeutic massage allows us to relax and release tension. Also, tell your doctor what you are going through so he or she can consider the implications while setting a strategy for your well-being. Our body, mind, and spirit will benefit from a holistic approach to health. Take care of yourself. Nurture your body with healthy meals, exercise, and plenty of sleep, because during this time your body will need the extra support.

Z Zero in on a cause and get involved. Regardless of your political preferences or on which side of an issue you may find yourself, use this opportunity to learn, discuss, and help make a difference. (Helpful hint: avoid getting obsessive or angry about the issue. Remember to keep it positive.) Short-term mission trips can be a great way to make a difference while being part of a team. Nothing builds our faith like being in a strange place with people we don't know, doing things we aren't very good at, and eating food we don't like while folks are speaking a language we don't understand. Stepping outside our comfort zone opens the door to see ourselves and our world in a fresh way, and we come back with new friends and great memories.

Notes

Chapter 1 The "Get Over It" Fallacy

1. *Good Morning America*, "National Get Over it Day," March 8, 2006.

2. Jeff Goldblatt, "Get Over It Day," www.getoveritday.com.

3. Michael Yaconelli, *Messy Spirituality* (Grand Rapids: Zondervan, 2002), 29.

Chapter 3 The Myth of Normal

1. Jaycee Dugard, *A Stolen Life* (New York: Simon & Schuster, 2011), 144–45.

2. Paul Tournier, MD, *The Strong and the Weak* (Philadelphia: Westminster Press, 1963), 20–21.

3. Oscar Wilde, *The Importance of Being Earnest: A Trivial Comedy for Serious People* (New York: Avon Publishers, 1976), Act II.

4. Brennan Manning, *Ruthless Trust: The Ragamuffin's Path to God* (San Francisco: HarperSanFrancisco, 2000), 122.

Chapter 4 The Joy of Depression

1. Jennifer Thomas, "Big Boys Do Cry," April 4, 2003, http://sci.rutgers.edu/forum/archive/index.php/t-22516.html.

2. Michael Hunt, "Big Boys Do Cry . . . Depression in Men," *Ingham Regional Medical Center Newsletter*, August 18, 2011.

3. Paul Zollo, "Bob Dylan 'Shoes for Everyone' Interview," *Bluerailroad—A Magazine of the Arts*, www.bluerailroad.wordpress.com. Featured in *Rolling Stone*, June 5, 1991.

4. Parker Posey, http://www.brainyquote.com/quotes/keywords/depression_2.html.

5. Gregory Jantz, *Moving Beyond Depression* (Colorado Springs: Shaw Publishers, 2003), 137.

6. Hunt, "Big Boys Do Cry . . . Depression in Men."

Chapter 5 It Can't Happen Here!

1. Elizabeth Kübler-Ross, *On Death and Dying* (New York: MacMillan, 1969).
2. C. S. Lewis, *A Grief Observed* (San Francisco: HarperSanFrancisco, 1961), 22.

Chapter 6 Fear

1. Henri Nouwen, *Making All Things New* (San Francisco: Harper & Row, 1981), 36.
2. Margarita Bertsos, "Shape Up! Daily Fitness Blog," May 28, 2008, http://www.glamour.com/health-fitness/blogs/shape-up/2008/05/do-the-thing-you-fear-most-and.html.

Chapter 7 Regret

1. Søren Kierkegaard, http://www.goodreads.com/author/quotes/6172.S_ren_Kierkegaard.
2. *Lord of the Rings: The Two Towers*, directed by Peter Jackson (New Line Cinema, 2002), DVD.
3. Alexander Graham Bell, "Thoughts on the Business of Life," Forbes.com/thoughts/opportunities/.

Chapter 8 Guilt

1. *Unforgiven*, directed by Clint Eastwood (1992; Warner Brothers, 1997), DVD.
2. Paul Tournier, *Guilt and Grace* (New York: Harper & Row, 1962), 23.

Chapter 10 Bitterness

1. Martin Luther King Jr., *Where Do We Go from Here: Chaos or Community?* (New York: Harper & Row, 1967), 62.
2. Shari Roan, "Bitterness as Mental Illness," *Los Angeles Times*, May 25, 2009.
3. Lewis Smedes, *Forgive & Forget* (New York: Harper & Row, 1984), 132–33.
4. Darrel Young, "Build a Wall," 2010. Used by permission.
5. Jon Krakauer, *Into the Wild* (New York: Anchor Books, 1996), 194.
6. Ibid.
7. *The Godfather*, directed by Francis Ford Coppola (1972; Paramount Pictures, 2008), DVD.
8. *Wayne's World*, directed by Penelope Spheeris (1992; Paramount Pictures, 2001), DVD.
9. Nelson Mandela, "Our March to Freedom Is Irreversible" (speech, February 11, 1990), http://en.wikisource.org/wiki/Nelson_Mandela's_address_on_his_release_from_prison.

Chapter 11 Life's Unfair—What Will We Do about It?

1. Michael Frost and Alan Hirsh, *The Shaping of Things to Come* (Sydney, Australia: Hendrikson, 2003), 1.

Chapter 12 Walking in the Light while Living in the Shadows

1. Emily Eaton, "Unfortunate or Privileged, Bad Stuff Happens to Everyone," July 4, 2011, creatingnewnormal.wordpress.com. See also www.juliangolden.com.

2. J. B. Phillips, *New Testament Christianity* (London: Hodder & Stoughton, 1958), 74.

Chapter 13 Glancing Back while Moving Forward

1. John Westfall and Bobbie Reed, *Building Strong People* (Grand Rapids: Baker, 1997).

2. Zev Wanderer and Tracy Cabot, *Letting Go* (New York: Bantam Books, 1978), 67.

3. Lewis Carroll, *Alice's Adventures in Wonderland* (New York: Signet Books, 1960), 47.

4. William Bridges, *Transitions* (Boston: Addison Wesley, 1980), 103.

5. Leo Tolstoy, *A Confession*, trans. Aylmer Maude (London: Oxford University Press, 1940).

6. Friedrich Nietzsche, *The Gay Science*, trans. W. Kaufmann (New York: Vintage Publishers, 1974), 283.

Dr. John Westfall is founding pastor of Harbor Church, a creative new congregation in the Pacific Northwest. He has pastored churches in Seattle, Washington; Walnut Creek, California; and Edina, Minnesota. John, an ordained pastor and an adjunct professor at Fuller Theological Seminary, is a popular conference speaker. He is author of *Coloring Outside the Lines* and *Enough Is Enough* and coauthor with Bobbie Reed of *Building Strong People*. John and his wife Eileen live in the Seattle area with Maggie, their Cavalier King Charles dog who probably has a personality disorder.

For information regarding retreats, seminars, and conferences, email John at dr.johnwestfall@gmail.com or visit his website at www.jwestfall.com.

Be the First
to Hear about
Other New Books
from Revell!

Sign up for announcements about new and upcoming titles at

www.revellbooks.com/signup

Follow us on
RevellBooks

Join us on
Revell

Don't miss out on our great reads!

℞
Revell
a division of Baker Publishing Group
www.RevellBooks.com